NARRATING UNEMPLOYMENT

For Susi

Narrating Unemployment

DOUGLAS EZZY
University of Tasmania

Ashgate

Aldershot • Burlington USA • Singapore • Sydney

© Douglas Ezzy 2001

Published by
Ashgate Publishing Limited
Gower House
Croft Road
Aldershot
Hampshire GU11 3HR
England

Ashgate Publishing Company
131 Main Street
Burlington, VT 05401-5600 USA

Ashgate website: http://www.ashgate.com

British Library Cataloguing in Publication Data
Ezzy, Douglas
    Narrating unemployment
    1. Unemployment 2. Unemployment - Social aspects
    I. Title
    331.1'37

Library of Congress Control Number: 2001093276

ISBN 0 7546 1528 6

Printed and bound in Great Britain by Biddles Ltd
www.biddles.co.uk

Contents

List of Figures and Tables

Acknowledgements

An earlier version of Chapter Two appeared as 'Unemployment and Mental Health: A Critical Review', *Social Science and Medicine*, 37: 41-52. Some sections of Chapter Three are drawn from 'Theorizing Narrative-Identity: Symbolic Interactionism and Hermeneutics' *The Sociological Quarterly*, 39: 239-252. Material from 'Fate and Agency in Job Loss Narratives' *Qualitative Sociology*, 23: 121-134 appears in a number of chapters. Chapter Eight draws on material from 'Subjectivity and the Labour Process: Conceptualising "Good Work"' *Sociology*, 31: 427-444. Finally, the methodological appendix includes material previously published in 'Lived Experience and Interpretation in Narrative Theory: Experiences of Living with HIV/AIDS' *Qualitative Sociology*, 21: 169-180. I acknowledge these journals for permission to reprint this material.

1 Introduction

Responses to unemployment vary from depression, through stoic acceptance, to celebration. The primary aim and original contribution of this book is to provide a sociological explanation for these variations. The different effects of unemployment are analysed as a product of the different types of stories people tell. Drawing on the traditions of symbolic interactionism and hermeneutics I use a narrative conception of self-identity to analyse people's stories about unemployment. Unemployment stories are in turn are a product of what happens to people, and how they react to what happens to them. This book examines the processes that allow some people to tell stories of hope and confidence about their unemployment, and lead other people to tell stories of pain, loss, and despair.

Most current studies of unemployment are either psychological or journalistic. The psychological studies have well developed theories of unemployment, but they typically rely on forced response questionnaires that do not allow unemployed people to speak for themselves. In contrast, the journalistic studies are often descriptively rich, but make little attempt to analyse the processes associated with unemployment. In this context, a study that both allows the unemployed to speak for themselves, and that draws on a sophisticated social psychological theory, is both timely and relevant to current debates in the unemployment literature.

The theories used to analyse the experience of unemployment in the psychological studies typically rely on simplified models of the person. These psychological models appear to ignore both the interpreted and temporal nature of human experience. An obsession with 'objective' measures has lead psychologists to ignore the way people interpret their experiences. Associated with this is an absence of any sophisticated analysis of how memories of the past and anticipations of the future influence unemployed people.

The study focuses on the experience of unemployment as a consequence of losing a job. This allows the temporal nature of unemployment to be examined more fully. In particular, it facilitates the examination of how events in the past are made sense of through stories told in the present that, in turn, describe a feared or desired future. The social psychological theory of narrative-identity developed in the book emphasises the temporal and interpreted nature of human

1

experience. The research explores in detail the influence of past experiences and imagined futures on the stories, or narrative-identities, of unemployed people. Further, I examine how stories about unemployment are influenced both by the 'objective' events of lived experience and their interpretation as part of 'subjective' narrative-identities. The explanation of the variations in the consequences of unemployment focuses on this dynamic interplay between the events of lived experience and their interpretation in a narrative.

A secondary aim of this study is to demonstrate the usefulness of a narrative conception of self-identity. While the self is socially and linguistically constructed, some deconstructionists have attempted to obliterate it, arguing that there is no such thing as a self. On the other hand, while the self is substantial and autonomous, it is not invulnerable and impermeable to social influences, as some psychologists appear to assume. The narrative theory utilised here charts a conception of the subject midway between these two extremes. The study of unemployment provides a concrete opportunity to assess and elaborate this theory of narrative-identity.

Similar to the everyday saying 'you don't realise how important something is until you've lost it', unemployment may be seen as a naturally occurring 'breach' (Garfinkel 1967) providing an important and otherwise rare perspective on the meaning of working. Responses to being without work expose the meaning of work in a new light because being *without* work makes the person more aware of the significance of her or his loss. A third aim of the study is, therefore, to examine the implications of the experience of unemployment for the meaning of working.

The meaning that an individual gives to working is framed by cultural expectations about working. Paid employment is typically understood as an integral part of becoming an independent adult in modern society. However, people do not always simply accept this cultural discourse, dutifully following the career recommended by their parents or their school Rather, individuals use and manipulate this discourse as they struggle to find employment that best serves their interests. Similarly, the organisation of society shapes the events of a person's life. However, individuals also actively construct their lives through the choices they make about the various courses of action open to them. A narrative conception of identity focuses on these processes that are integral to the construction of the meaning of working and unemployment.

Qualitative interviews provide an excellent method for examining these issues. The empirical research is designed to assess and expand the theory developed in the earlier Chapters of the study. The descriptive

Chapters report the fruits of this research, demonstrating that a sociological conception of the narrative self provides a rich, subtle and incisive framework for the analysis of the experience of unemployment. A qualitative methodology is the most appropriate for investigating these issues. Hammarstrom and Janlert (1997:294) observe that 'most unemployment research has been based on quantitative methods, and has not always provided a deep understanding of what it means to be unemployed or shed much light on mediating mechanisms or theoretical models'.

The value of qualitative research is underlined by Payne (1994) who provides a telling critique of a book summarising the findings from a very large longitudinal quantitative study of youth unemployment in Australia (Winefield et al. 1993). She notes 'the study collected no contextual data, and only the briefest details of respondents' actual experience of employment and unemployment; as a result interpretation is difficult' (Payne 1994:712). While large quantitative studies have their place, allowing results to be generalised to larger populations, on their own they do not provide a sophisticated understanding of the experience of unemployment.

A detailed critical review of existing theoretical explanations of the social psychological consequences of unemployment is provided in Chapter Two. Theories reviewed include the rehabilitation approach, the stages model, Jahoda's functional model, Warr's vitamin model and Fryer's agency critique. Most theories are found to deal inadequately with the temporal aspects of unemployment and the relationship between subjective experience and objective location.

Chapter Three outlines a narrative theory of self-identity, providing the theoretical background to the research. The Chapter synthesises three distinct theoretical traditions concerned with the self-concept: Ricoeur's hermeneutic theory of self-identity as a narrative; symbolic interactionist analysis of the intersubjective sources of the self and the theory of status passage; and social constructionism's theorising of the narrative formation of self-evaluations. While a narrative-identity configures lived experience, it is not determined by it. The focus of the study is on the interaction between the events of a job loss status passage and their configuration in a narrative or story. Specifically, different self-evaluative consequences of job loss can be understood as a product of different stories used to narrate the job loss passage.

The next four Chapters of the study report the inductively derived findings of qualitative research. The methodology utilised for the research is described in the Appendix. Three main types of job loss are identified: romances, tragedies, and more complex experiences.

Chapter Four describes romantic narratives that portray job loss as a moment of liberation from an oppressive occupation. Unemployment is experienced as liberating and as a valued opportunity. Two sub-types of romantic narratives are identified. Strong romances provide a long term plan for the future through the development of an alternative career. On the other hand, in weak romances unemployment is portrayed as a holiday. Weak romances do not provide a long term plan and have the potential to become tragedies.

Tragic narratives of job loss have two distinct phases: separation and liminality, described in Chapters Five and Six respectively. Chapter Five recounts how the separation involved in tragic job loss undermines a person's social relationships and their[1] life plan. Life plans typically involve a secure, well paid, enjoyable job that people envision as enabling them to achieve a variety of other desired goals. Job loss renders this narrated life plan implausible. It is this discrepancy between an ideal life plan and what people fear might happen as a consequence of their job loss that is the main source of depression and anxiety described in tragic narratives. I identify four sub-types of tragic job loss narratives: traumatic tragedies, moderated tragedies, ironic tragedies, and sustained tragedies.

Chapter Six examines the experience of being unemployed after a tragic job loss. This form of unemployment leaves a person in a liminal, or in-between, phase defined by a feeling of exclusion from work and society more generally. Three types of responses may occur during liminal unemployment: searching for employment, participation in alternative activities that give structure to the day, and periods of resignation to unemployment associated with severe depression. These different responses are a product of the interaction of the events of lived experience and their interpretation in a narrative.

In some interview narratives the consequence of a job loss is determined by events in non-work roles such as a marital breakdown or a serious illness. This is examined in Chapter Seven. The events in non-work roles involve 'complicating passages' that are more influential

---

[1]   While sexist language is generally easily avoided, sometimes this can result in cumbersome and confusing sentence construction. Throughout this book, when discussing what "a person" in the abstract might do or think, I refer to "their" actions or thoughts. While technically "their" is a plural form of the third person pronoun, I use "their" as a non-sexist singular form of the third person pronoun. This seems less obtrusive than other alternatives such as repeatedly referring to "his or her" actions or attitudes, using "his/her," or sometimes making the abstract person a female and sometimes a male.

on a person's self-evaluation than the events associated with the job loss passage. The meaning of working, and therefore of unemployment, develops out of a person's narrative interpretation of their life as a whole. This Chapter underlines the point that work is not always the central, or dominant, influence on a person's life.

As argued earlier, job loss is a form of breaching experiment that exposes the significance of working life and this is examined in Chapter Eight. First, some recent studies of the construction of subjectivity in the work place are reviewed. While cultural discourses about the importance of having a career shape a person's self-narrative, they do not determine self-understandings. People also creatively use these discourses to construct novel interpretations of their experiences. However, structural changes to the organisation of work in modern society are changing the availability of certain types of jobs, that in turn shapes common experiences of work. The Chapter argues that people's ability to be agents, and respond creatively to unemployment, is at least in part shaped by their social location and access to financial and cultural resources.

The final Chapter reviews the main themes and conclusions of the study. I summarise the conception of self-identity as constructed in a narrative and its application to the analysis of job loss. This understanding is compared to other studies of unemployment, and its implications outlined. Finally I comment on some potential future directions for the study of subjectivity, unemployment and the meaning of working.

2 Unemployment and Mental Health: A Critical Review

Introduction

It is now clear that the relationship between employment status and self-evaluation is complex and subtle. Simplistic identifications of work as 'good' and unemployment as 'bad' are manifestly inadequate as explanations of observed variations in the effects of unemployment on self-evaluations. This inadequacy is clear even at the most basic level: while the majority of people who become unemployed report increased distress and anxiety, there are also a substantial minority who report feeling happier and relieved when they become unemployed. Similarly, while re-employment typically restores original self-evaluations, some re-employed people report increased distress and anxiety. The central question that this Chapter addresses is: What explanations have been given for the variations in the self-evaluative consequences of unemployment?

The Chapter is divided into three main sections. First, I provide a brief, critical summary of current research into the social psychological effects of unemployment. This provides the rationale for the rest of the Chapter. Second, I review existing theories that purport to explain variations in the self-evaluative consequences of unemployment. Finally, drawing on narrative theory, I suggest an alternative conceptualisation of job loss as a type of status passage.

A Critical Overview of the Unemployment Literature

The negative consequences of unemployment were first described in the 1930s by researchers such as Jahoda, Lazarsfeld and Zeisel (1933), Bakke (1934) and Komarovsky (1940). Based on a wide variety of qualitative and quantitative research these studies provide detailed and sensitive insights into the meaning and experience of unemployment. Although there were no established scales of mental health in the 1930s, the general experience of the unemployed was clearly an unpleasant one and psychologically destructive. Recent research has demonstrated in more rigorous quantitative terms that, independent of previous levels of mental health, losing a job typically results in reduced levels of psychological well-being compared to control groups who retain employment (Winefield 1995). Although recent studies also include some excellent examples of qualitative research rich in descriptive detail (Burman 1988; Marsden and Duff 1975; Seabrook 1982), most research has been conducted using quantitative methodologies and oriented toward testing various psychological and psychiatric effects amongst the unemployed (for example Feather 1990; O'Brien 1986; Warr 1987).

Unemployment is not always negative, and employment is not always positive (Fineman 1983; Fryer and Payne 1986; O'Brien 1986). Bakke (1934) first observed that some people became adapted to being unemployed. These people found unemployment more pleasant than employment because they could only gain work in oppressive occupations where monetary rewards were barely greater than those gained from social welfare. More recent empirical research demonstrates that the experience of the unemployed varies considerably depending on a variety of factors including: the person's age, gender, income, social support, reason for job loss, commitment to employment, satisfaction with previous work, expectation of returning to work and length of unemployment (see Winefield 1995 for an exhaustive review). These factors are said to 'moderate' the typically negative consequences of unemployment. For example, the greater the employment commitment of an individual, the stronger the negative effects of unemployment on mental health and self-esteem. While there is still some debate over the strength of the effects of some of these variables and ongoing refinements in the exact nature of the relationships, in most cases the general direction of the effect is reasonably clear. Although no one study has included all of these factors, their combination has resulted in a complex picture of the social psychology of unemployment.

While the *descriptive* picture is complex and well documented, the *explanations* for these effects are typically far from elaborate. When moderating effects are identified it is often unclear why they have the effect they do. Explanations are typically *ad hoc* and *post facto* rather than theoretically derived from empirical research. As Hartley and Fryer note:

> It is not clear whether moderator variables, if they are indeed influential, reflect variation in the objective circumstances of unemployment or whether they influence social psychological factors operating at the individual level, and this is not discussed to any great extent. For example, age could be a sociological shorthand, signalling variation in the objective opportunities existing in the labour market (an older worker is less attractive to employers) or else age may represent a psychological dimension of mental flexibility, risk-taking propensity,

domestic involvement and so forth. This is true for many of the so-called mediating variables. (Hartley and Fryer 1984:19)

This lack of explanation is in large part a consequence of a lack of a general theory under which the available knowledge of the social psychological effects of employment and unemployment could be integrated. Kabanoff (1982) recalls that Eisenberg and Lazarsfeld (1938) observed that there was no general theoretical scheme guiding analyses of unemployment. He goes on to argue that 'it is my impression that we are again seeing a mass of interesting but piecemeal research that does not have an overall problem network into which to fit itself' (Kabanoff 1982:37).

A large number of reviewers have pointed out that a significant portion of existing studies of unemployment are almost entirely descriptive (Carr-Hill 1984; Feather and O'Brien 1986; Hartley and Fryer 1984; Jahoda 1988; Kabanoff 1982; Kelvin and Jarret 1985; Warr 1987). This is not to suggest that descriptive accounts have no value, on the contrary, they form the basis for building more general theoretical analyses. Rather, the problem is that given that the experiences of the unemployed have now been extensively charted, there is an increasing need for links between these descriptive accounts and more general social psychological theory.

Jahoda (1981:184) argues that this mismatch between research and theoretical explanations is 'as it must be' due to the impossibility of developing a comprehensive theory for even a limited part of a field as wide as morale and work. However, Jahoda's point is more directly applicable to 'grand theory' - a label applied by Mills (1970) to sociological theories that attempt to create universal schemes to explain the continuing existence of society. As Jahoda's own attempt to develop a theory of unemployment demonstrates, a much more useful level of theorising is that of the 'middle range' (Merton 1968). Middle range theory is that which lies between simple empiricist hypothesis and grand theory, it aims at describing and explaining a small section of social reality. The descriptive emphasis of much of the unemployment literature has meant that there are only a few studies that attempt to develop a middle range level explanation of the social psychological processes associated with unemployment. There is therefore a clear need for analyses informed by more general theoretical models of the relationship between employment status and self-evaluations. This Chapter outlines and assesses existing theories and suggests an alternative theory of job loss as a status passage and self-identity as a narrative.

Models of the Social Psychological Effects of Unemployment

Despite the dominance of descriptive studies, there are a number of models or theories that have been developed to explain the self-evaluative consequences of unemployment. This section critically reviews these models. The order of presentation is roughly in line with the degree of sophistication of the models and also, to some extent, follows their chronological appearance, some later models being developed in response to earlier ones. The models are as follows: the rehabilitation approach, the stages model, Jahoda's functional model, Warr's vitamin model, O'Brien's analysis of personal control, Feather's expectancy-value theory, and Fryer's agency restriction approach. In each case I summarise the model, suggest some important criticisms, and attempt to evaluate the adequacy of the model as an explanation of the observed variations in the effects of unemployment on self-evaluations.

The 'Rehabilitation' Approach

Perhaps the most problematic explanation for the negative effects of unemployment is that used by a variety of studies that can be subsumed under the generic description of rehabilitation approaches. Tiffany, Cowan and Tiffany (1970), a typical study in this genre, argue that the greater proportion of the unemployed are unemployed for psychological reasons: 'they show avoidance behaviour patterns or what has been referred to as "work inhibition", which implies that the are physically capable of work but are prevented from working because of psychological disabilities' (Tiffany et al. 1970:15). The appropriate response of the state to the unemployed is therefore to rehabilitate them through providing therapy or training to rectify their lack of responsibility and self control.

The rehabilitationist interpretation has many similarities with the distinction made in the thirteenth century between the 'deserving poor' and the 'sturdy beggar', the former unable to work due to physical disabilities, the latter, though able bodied, do not work and are lazy, and therefore do not deserve any assistance. This distinction was formulated in the year after the black death when there was an exceptional shortage of labour and it still influences language used today to describe the unemployed (Kelvin 1984).

Most studies within the rehabilitationist genre have also been conducted during times of relatively low unemployment rates. Within this sampling context it is therefore not surprising that Tiffany and his associates' research, for example, conducted during the relative prosperity of the late sixties in America, should point toward more individualistic and less structural reasons for unemployment. On the other hand, most other sociological and psychological studies of unemployment have been conducted during times when unemployment rates are much higher, typically during economic downturns. At these times a much higher proportion of unemployment can be attributed to 'structural' causes than during times of economic prosperity.

However, even given the historical setting of the rehabilitation psychologists' studies, such a person centred approach is inadequate not only because it smacks of the 'blaming the victim' syndrome, but because it locates the problem in the individual, not in the relationship between the objective social location and individual responses to this (O'Brien 1986). Miles (1987) describes this tendency as the 'medicalisation' of research into unemployment. The danger associated with this is clearest in the case of health professionals who have a propensity to see unemployment related problems isolated from their social roots: 'They may see unemployment as a personal characteristic that renders the individual prone to illness, rather than as a social process adding to the risk factors in peoples lives' (Miles, 1987:223). Thus rehabilitation approaches, similar to the human relations approach in the study of work itself, leave untouched the conditions of employment and other social aspects that are instrumental in producing negative self-evaluations and low mental health.

Even recent studies conducted during times of high unemployment appear to advocate policies that smack of the victim blaming characteristic of the rehabilitation approach. Winefield and associates (1993:90), for example, conclude their Chapter on 'Coping with Unemployment' with the suggestion that young unemployed people should be 'counselled to engage in purposeful activities' and to avoid watching TV. This suggestion is not only paternalistic, and unlikely to be taken seriously by unemployed people, it also demonstrates a failure to understand the social and cultural sources of depression amongst those unemployed people who are inactive or watch television.

From a broader social structural perspective, rather than viewing the unemployed as deficient or inadequate, it may be more appropriate to see them as unwitting and unwilling sacrifices to the prosperity of others. In other words, their deficiency or inadequacy can be seen as located in inequitable social relationships and the structural constraints that cause unemployment. Illustrations of this can be found equally in the seventeenth century practice of 'enclosure' that deprived peasants of their land resulting in mass unemployment and in more recent monetarist policies which target inflation rather than unemployment: 'the former being more injurious to capital accumulation than the latter' (Burman 1988:11).

With regard to the question of explaining the variations in the mental health consequences of unemployment, the rehabilitationist approach simplifies and caricatures the diversity and complexity of the experience of the unemployed. It lacks sophistication and, given that some people might have an aversion to employment, the theory fails to consider why people should come to have such difficulties with working.

The Stages Model

The most influential statement of the unemployment stages or phases model is usually attributed to Eisenberg and Lazarsfeld (1938), although it is also discussed by Bakke (1933) and Jahoda and her associates (1933). Based on a wide ranging review of research on unemployment available in the 1930s Eisenberg and Lazarsfeld suggest a three stage model:

> First there is shock, which is followed by an active hunt for a job, during which the individual is still optimistic and unresigned; he [sic.] still maintains an unbroken attitude. Second, when all efforts fail, the individual becomes pessimistic, anxious, and suffers active distress; this is the most crucial state of all. And third, the individual becomes fatalistic and adapts himself to his new state but with a narrower scope. He now has a broken attitude. (Eisenberg and Lazarsfeld 1938:378)

Similarly, Jahoda, Lazarsfeld and Zeisel (1933) in their study of *Marienthal*, a village in Austria with abnormally high unemployment during the depression in the early 1930s, distinguished four types of basic attitudes amongst the unemployed: resignation, unbroken, despair, and apathetic. More recently there have appeared some reports of studies that support various versions of the stage model (Hepworth 1980; Hayes and Nutman 1981; Warr and Jackson 1983). For example, Hill (1978), on the basis of a large British survey of unemployed youth, has identified a three stage model of the responses to unemployment: a period of optimism is followed by increasing stress that leads into a state of toleration and depression.

The conviction that the response to stressful events takes the form of a progression through stages is widespread in psychology, particularly in fields such as dying, bereavement, retirement, and career change (Brown 1990; Kearl 1987; Kubler-Ross 1969). The assumption that psychological responses to significant events should change over time also has considerable initial plausibility. However, there are a number of serious methodological and theoretical problems with stage accounts.

Fryer (1985) has argued that the empirical evidence supporting stage accounts of the response to unemployment is often methodologically problematic, plagued by internal contradictions and the use of extremely plastic and flexible categories. Many cross-sectional studies have failed to demonstrate an association between duration of unemployment and psychological well-being (Warr and Jackson 1983; Fryer 1985:268; Archer and Rhodes 1987). On the basis of a longitudinal study, Stokes and Cochrane (1984:309) expressly report that their results 'fail to support the stages model of unemployment'. Further, studies that do identify stages produce contradictory models that are only reconcilable in an extremely general sense and are of very limited use for the purposes of explanation.

The stages model is not so much a theory as a descriptive framework, the operational variable being length of unemployment. Stages accounts do not *explain* the 'patterns' as a theory should, they merely assert that they are there. The problematic nature of stage theories that simplify the experience of the person going through the passage has also been noted in other substantive areas (for a review of the problems associated with stage accounts of bereavement see Archer and Rhodes 1987). Kellehear (1990:20), with reference to dying in particular and stages theory in general, points out that:

> A theory which encourages the view of one developmental path in matters of conduct allows exceptions to be labelled as deviant, abnormal or dysfunctional. There is a danger that cultural differences will be rationalised as personal inadequacy. Furthermore, there is the risk of professional misreading of description as prescription.

To attempt to identify stages on the basis of aggregated survey results that do not take into account the systematic variations in the effect of unemployment is to treat the unemployed as a homogenous group. This assumption of homogeneity ignores, and definitely does not explain, the experiences of a large number of the unemployed who do not follow the identified 'pattern'.

There is some evidence of stages in response to unemployment, particularly for a final stage of fatalism and apathy (Kelvin and Jarret 1985:26). However, the problems in methodology, ambiguous and ambivalent denotation of stages, normative bias, simplification of the experience of the unemployed, and the lack of true theoretical explanation suggest that stage accounts are not particularly useful frameworks to explain the complexity of the experiences of the unemployed.

Jahoda's Functional Model

Perhaps the most commonly referred to explanation for the deleterious effects of unemployment is Marie Jahoda's functional model (Jahoda 1981; 1982; 1984; 1986; 1988). Jahoda's central contention is that unemployment deprives an individual of various beneficial by-products typically gained from employment. Making use of Merton's (1968) functional paradigm, Jahoda differentiates between manifest and latent functions of employment.

The manifest and generally taken for granted consequence of employment is financial remuneration, allowing an individual to 'earn a living'. Further, Jahoda argues that people derive five ties from employment as latent by-products:

> First, employment imposes a time structure on the working day; second, employment implies regularly shared experiences and contacts with people outside the nuclear family; third, employment links individuals to goals and purposes that transcend their own; fourth employment defines aspects of personal status and identity; and finally, employment enforces activity. (Jahoda 1981:188)

According to Jahoda's account it is these 'objective' latent consequences, not purposefully planned, which explain the motivation to work in modern society and help to explain why 'employment is psychologically supportive even when conditions are bad' (Jahoda 1981:188). On the other hand, unemployment is psychologically destructive due to the absence of these latent functions. Jahoda also points out that leisure, because it lacks the manifest and most of the latent functions of work, cannot provide a 'functional alternative' to employment (Jahoda 1981:189).

For Jahoda it is not just the economic deprivation of unemployment that results in the negative mental health consequences of unemployment - because unemployment also affects the financially secure. Rather, she argues that the experience which 'all those who lost jobs have in common is the abrupt exclusion from a social institution that had previously dominated their daily lives' (Jahoda 1988:17).

The functional explanation is derived from an analysis of the fit or misfit between socially imposed experiences and human needs. On the social dimension, participation in the institution of employment is the major support for workers' psychological well being. Complementary to this Jahoda suggests a set of 'psychological needs' relevant to being employed: 'people need some structure to the waking day, need an enlarged horizon beyond their primary group, need to be involved in collective efforts, need to know where they stand in society and need to be active' (Jahoda 1986:26). The negative psychological effects of unemployment can therefore be explained as a consequence of the individual's exclusion from an institution that meets basic psychological needs. Jahoda suggests that the fact that there is a minority who do not suffer when unemployed is a product of their having found niches in institutions that provide functional alternatives to employment and which meet the same set of needs (Jahoda 1984; 1986).

However, the suggestion that mental health is simply a product of whether institutional engagements meet individual needs is problematic. The approach ignores the interpretative process of individuals undergoing the experience of becoming unemployed. This problem becomes particularly obvious in attempting to explain differences in the experiences of the unemployed. Why is it, for example, that age is curvilinearly related to the effects of unemployment with older and younger people reporting less severe effects that people in between? The functional approach does not suggest a mechanism to account for such variations in the effects of unemployment on self concept and mental health.

Empirical studies have in addition demonstrated both that people leaving dissatisfying and stressful work often welcome unemployment as a relief and report improved psychological well being (Graetz 1990; Fineman 1983:134) and that re-employment in a dissatisfying job does not reverse the negative effects of unemployment (Graetz 1990; O'Brien and Feather 1990; Winefield et al. 1990). However, the functionalist theory is unable to account for these effects. While Jahoda is aware that much contemporary work is repetitive, boring, low skilled and detrimental to psychological well being (Jahoda 1982:24), her theoretical assumptions emphasise the experience of the unemployed in terms of lack of time structure, social purpose, and meaningful activity. 'They do not lead to any consideration of how past employment modifies or even determines adjustment to unemployment' (O'Brien 1985:890). This neglect of work content also stems in part from Jahoda linking her theory into Freud's description of work as a person's strongest tie to reality (Jahoda 1981:188). From this point of view, the five latent consequences Jahoda identifies can be seen as an elaboration of how work ties the person to reality. The degree to which the 'ties to reality' provided by employment are pleasurable is only a secondary consideration: 'even unpleasant ties to reality are preferable to their absence' (Jahoda 1981:189).

Jahoda appears to romanticise employment and fails to appreciate that paid employment is, for some people, isolating and unpleasant, providing little in the ways of 'ties to reality'. It is a highly dubious proposition that the conditions of employment characteristic of modern capitalistic society should be universally conducive to positive psychological well-being. This proposition perhaps reflects the middle-class occupations of researchers rather than the experiences of many unemployed people (Hartley and Fryer 1984:20). Empirical studies concerning the effects of work conditions on mental health demonstrate that there are significant minorities who find their job oppressive and alienating (Kohn and Schooler 1983; Meaning of Work Research Group 1987). Winefield (1995) points out that a large number of psychological studies have consistently found that those who regarded their jobs as 'unsatisfactory' reported mental health levels no different to people who were unemployed. Further, the proposition is inconsistent with general sociological theorising on the meaning of work as exemplified by Marx who argued that most work in modern society is alienating and destructive of the self.

There is a large sociological literature concerned with the meaning of work and its variable significance for the individual (see Rose 1989 and Kohn and Schooler 1983 for reviews). However, such references only rarely appear in the literature on unemployment. This may in part be a product of the psychological orientation of much of the research concerning unemployment. I suggest that these concerns are central to an understanding of the variations in the effects of unemployment and should be integrated into a theory of the effects of unemployment on self-evaluations. For example, variation in the degree of attachment to paid labour has been used by Rowley and Feather (1987) to explain age differences in people's responses to unemployment. Other variations in the effect of unemployment may be similarly explained as a consequence of associated variations in the meaning of work (Hakim 1983).

Jahoda has identified some important characteristics of the institution of employment that appear to be supportive of psychological well-being for a portion of the employed. Particularly useful, I suggest, are the dimensions of people's experiences that are identified as influencing psychological well being. However, the functional theory fails to take into account either the differences in the experiences at work or the variations in the meaning unemployment may have depending on an individual's social location. One attempt to develop the functional model to account for these differences is Warr's (1987) 'vitamin model'.

Warr's Vitamin Model

Drawing on medical terminology Warr (1987) suggests that analogous to
the effect of vitamins on physical health, various environmental factors
are influential on mental health. More specifically, Warr identifies nine
environmental features or 'vitamins' that are assumed to be of importance
in determining mental health. These environmental features are:
opportunity for control, opportunity for skill use, externally generated
goals, variety, environmental clarity, availability of money, physical
security, opportunity for interpersonal contact, and valued social position.

The central contention of this model is that when levels of
environmental 'vitamins' are low, this will result in lowered levels of
mental health. The vitamin model is 'situation-centred' in that it focuses
on the characteristics of the environment rather than the experience of
the person. However, Warr also describes the model as 'enabling' because
'people are assumed to be able to shape the character of their environment
and to influence its impact upon them' (Warr 1987:22).

The vitamin model provides standardised evaluation criteria for
describing the environments of different jobs and various situations of
the unemployed. In the case of the unemployed, the nine categories can
be used to describe the magnitude of the change between the employed
and unemployed environments. The commonly observed negative impact
of unemployment can therefore be explained in terms of the impoverished
environment of the unemployed.

In contrast to Jahoda's functional model, the vitamin model can
account for the observed positive effects of leaving oppressive work and
the negative effects of becoming employed in dissatisfying work. These
are explained with reference to the relative differences in the environments
of unemployment and employment. That is to say, an oppressive work
environment may contain less 'vitamins' than the unemployed
environment, the movement into the relatively more 'healthy'
environment of unemployment would therefore be expected to result in
improved psychological well-being.

Further, the observed differences in mental health amongst other
subgroups of the unemployed can be similarly explained in terms of
variations in the environments of these subgroups. For example,
unemployment for middle aged men results in much greater problems
with availability of money, security, opportunities for personal contact
and valued social position than does unemployment for teenagers, who
are typically relatively less dependent on work for adequate levels of
many of these 'vitamins'.

An excellent example of the utility of Warr's model is provided by Jackson's (1999) study of psychosocial experiences amongst a small (N=127) sample of Canadian young adults. Consistent with Warr's vitamin model, Jackson found that, compared to employed respondents, unemployed respondents scored significantly lower on indicators of the nine 'vitamins'. Further, students scored higher than unemployed people, but not as highly as employed people. 'The findings provide additional support for contextual models of mental health and suggest that full-time education partially buffers the negative psychological consequences of unemployment when opportunities for employment are absent' (Jackson 1999:49).

Warr's explanation of different levels of mental health amongst the unemployed in terms of different environments goes well beyond Jahoda's dichotomous characterisation of work and unemployment. Warr is also concerned to include the effect of people's orientations to their environment, particularly focusing on the moderating effects of baseline mental health. People with high baseline mental health are affected less by low environmental vitamins than people with low baseline mental health.

Many of the environmental features identified by Warr are common to Jahoda's analysis of the functions of employment: financial rewards, social contacts, social purposes, and status and identity. One critical addition made by Warr is that of 'opportunity for control' and the related 'opportunity for skill use'. However, Jahoda (1986) has also noted that the dimension of control was a significant omission from her original list.

A significant difference between Jahoda's model and Warr's vitamin model is the intended generality of application. Jahoda's analysis is explicitly limited to the benefits of employment, although she does suggest that participation in other institutions may provide 'functional alternatives'. Warr, on the other hand, suggests that the identified features can be used to assess the effects of a wide range of environments on mental health. However, what the vitamin model gains in generality of application, it loses in depth of analysis. Jahoda's framework provides a basis for more incisive insight into the experience of the unemployed, their frustrations and the pressures that motivate people to search for work. Warr explicitly limits his analysis to effects on mental health.

Warr's vitamin model has a number of other limitations. First, although Warr (1987:20) suggests that the model could be applied to analysing the mental health effects of changes in other arenas, he only applies it to the analysis of work and unemployment. The argument for the theory, as a general theory, lacks the comparative basis that would support such a claim. Second, the explicit limitation of consideration to the effects of unemployment on mental health suggests an implicit, though probably unintended message that other aspects of the experience of the unemployed are not significant. The lost opportunities, shattered trust and disenchantment of the unemployed are not discussed. Finally, and most importantly, Warr's theory is limited in that it does not explicitly and systematically deal with the interaction between a person's social environment and the meanings and interpretations of the experiencing individual within this environment.

The problematic nature of Warr's exclusion of subjective orientations is perhaps most clear when considering moderating variables associated with variations in the meaning of work. One important, empirically identified, moderator is a dispositional variable variously termed 'employment commitment' or the 'Protestant work ethic' (Jackson et al. 1983).[2] Typically, the greater the commitment to employment, the stronger the negative effects of unemployment. Warr's discussion of employment commitment appears to reinterpret it in terms of its relationship to environmental factors (Warr 1987:225-226). This is an unconvincing and unsatisfactory attempt to integrate employment commitment systematically into the vitamin model. While people's commitment to work is shaped by and also shapes their environment, it is not the environment, but the subjective meaning of employment that is the empirically significant variable.

Warr's account of how differences in environments influence mental health often appears to derive plausibility from an implicit suggestion that it is the interpretation individual's give to their environments that results in changed levels of mental health (for example Warr 1987:212-222). However, people's interpretation of their situation is not at all part of Warr's formal theory. Warr is aware of this inadequacy (Warr 1987:19, 271), and towards the end of his book he attempts to justify a situation centred approach arguing that little research has been done on interactions between situation and person in the field of unemployment.

---

2   Discussions of employment commitment are often linked to Weber's analysis of the Protestant work ethic (for example Walker et al. 1984; Kelvin 1981). However, such analyses often seem to misunderstand Weber's argument, wrongly denying its validity (for a particularly bad example see Kelvin and Jarret 1985:100-108). Some researchers seem to think that Weber argued that a substantial body of the working class continues to work out of a sense of religious calling. However, Weber (1976) argues that orientations toward work are influenced by a secularised form of the Protestant work ethic. The "spirit of capitalism" does not involve a desire to work motivated by a sense of religious calling, but its secularised descendent - where work as a duty and obligation are central to the individual's conception of living.

He suggests this is due to both empirical difficulties in gaining independent measures of situations and persons, and due to the lack of a developed theory incorporating both types of variables. This second point is taken up later in the Chapter.

O'Brien's Analysis of Personal Control

O'Brien (1985) takes the analysis of agency a step further through an examination of the relationship between previous working conditions and a sense of personal control. Drawing on a re-analysis of Bakke's studies of unemployment during the 1930s O'Brien points out that 'many of the characteristics commonly attributed to the unemployed such as apathy, depression, and external control were often due to the combined effects of past work experience and economic deprivation' (O'Brien 1985:877). The personal powerlessness of the unemployed did not derive only from a mood change associated with unemployment but from their prior employment experience. Most of the unemployed were from working class backgrounds and Bakke observed that the life of the employed working class person is characterised by a feeling that destinies are controlled by people and forces outside their realm of experience. 'Habit breeds attitudes. When so much of your life is ordered by others why pretend to be able to do anything yourself with the rest?' (Bakke 1934:10).

Although Bakke does not present a formally stated theory of personality, he does consistently emphasise that task experiences and income mould personality. One major dimension of personality identified is that of locus of control. O'Brien suggests at least three categories of control that can be usefully distinguished in describing how individuals respond to unemployment: internals, externals, and realistics (O'Brien 1985:888). Thus, an analysis of the effect of job content on personal control provides a theoretical mechanism for explaining patterns of unemployment behaviour. For example, when work has fostered a sense of personal control, behaviour during unemployment reflects this greater sense of personal efficacy.

This form of theorising moves away from the more static, exclusively psychological or purely environmental frameworks to a more biographical approach. It places emphasis on the longer term continuities in an individual's self-concept that mediate the impact of changes in an individual's environment as a consequence of unemployment. However, O'Brien develops only one aspect of this biographical approach, that of personal control. I suggest that this framework can be broadened to include both dimensions of individual orientations and social situational pressures on the individual other than the work environment. I expand on this explanation later in the Chapter.

Feather's Expectancy-Value Theory

Feather and associates (Feather and Davenport 1981; Feather 1990; Feather 1992) have argued that variations in the depressive effects among the unemployed are related to variations in expectations and values. For example, in a cross sectional study Feather and Davenport (1981) found that unemployed youth tended to be more depressed if they reported highly valuing having a job and had a higher expectancy of obtaining employment. That is to say, if an unemployed person wants to work and expects that they should be able to obtain work, they tend to be more depressed than an unemployed person who does not really want to work and does not really expect to find work. Attribution of the cause of unemployment is also linked to the level of depression among the unemployed. Higher levels of depression was correlated with external attribution in which the unemployed person absolved themselves of the blame for their unemployed status (Feather and Davenport 1981).

Feather's theory utilises an model of the person as an active agent, 'appraising and construing situations in terms of available alternative courses of action and assessing the likelihood that actions can be performed and that these actions will lead to affectively toned outcomes and consequences' (Feather 1992:317). In particular, Feather emphasises the role of values and expectations in shaping how unemployed people act, including job-seeking behaviour.

The social and cultural sources of the variations in people's expectations and values are implicit in the theory, however, they are not clearly theorised. Feather (1992), for example, reports that expectations are a product of an individual's beliefs about a variety of social dimensions, including the success of other job seekers, the level of competition in the labour market, and the unemployed person's assessment of their relative skill levels. However, the social processes that generate these beliefs are not explored empirically, nor are they adequately theorised. Similarly, the role of 'the environment' in expectancy-value theory suggests, but insufficiently theorises the importance of social factors:

> The economic deprivation that the unemployed person experiences creates a psychological environment in which goal-directed activity is blocked and frustrated because opportunities to satisfy or fulfil important motives are limited. Over time, these restrictions may take their toll in reduced psychological

health, in negative views of the self, in low expectations concerning goal attainment and personal capabilities, and in behavioural deficits. (Feather 1997:42)

Expectancy-value theory focuses on the goal directed behaviours of unemployed people. As a consequence Feather (1992) argues that it is most usefully applied to the analysis of job-seeking behaviour rather than more general psychological well-being. However, Feather's attempt to apply the theory to subjective well-being does indicate the complex interweaving of past social experience, present values, and anticipated outcomes. In other words, expectancy-value theory highlights the integrally temporal nature of both self-understanding and the interpretative process used by unemployed people to make sense of their experience.

Expectancy-value theory indicates the importance of both the temporal nature, and the social sources, of the psychological consequences of unemployment. Feather has also highlighted the role of causal attributions in shaping people's response to unemployment. However, the model of the person utilised by this theory remains mechanistic, overly rational, and undersocialised.

Fryer's Agency Critique

Both Jahoda's functional model and Warr's vitamin model fail to deal with the interpretation of unemployment as seen from the perspective of the unemployed themselves. While O'Brien's and Feather's theories both attempt to address this issue, perhaps the most sophisticated analysis has been developed by Fryer and his associates (Fryer 1986; 1992; 1995; Fryer and Payne 1984; 1986; Hartley and Fryer 1984). Arguing from the standpoint of a cognitively oriented psychology Fryer develops a critique of the predominant presupposition of a passive actor in unemployment research.

Fryer recognises that employment plays an important supportive role and that the loss of employment can have deleterious consequences. However, he suggests that at least equally as important are the problems associated with being unemployed and 'the contribution which is brought to the social situation of unemployment by the experiencing agent in terms of beliefs, intentions, and goals for self-actualisation' (Fryer 1986:236).

To illustrate this point, Fryer and Payne (1984) present data from semi-structured interviews with 11 'proactive' unemployed people in the United Kingdom. They use 'proactive' to denote an agent who 'chooses to take the lead, initiate and intervene in situations to bring about change in valued directions rather than responding to imposed change passively' (Fryer and Payne 1984:285). The proactive unemployed people interviewed, though experiencing material privation as a result of unemployment, were not experiencing psychological deprivation. This was primarily due to active participation in a number of voluntary organisations. The subjects are reported to have distinguished work, as a purposeful activity, from employment, as a social institution. This enabled them to 'exploit the opportunity to work even though the possibility of employment is denied to them or rejected by them' (Fryer and Payne 1984:285). On the basis of this data, and as an alternative to Jahoda's passive model, Fryer and Payne (1984:287) suggest a view of the person as an 'active social agent striving to make sense of his or her situation and acting according to reasons and intentions to pursue chosen goals'.

Further, Fryer (1992; 1995) argues that when unemployed people do become distressed, that this is a product of unemployment restricting their agency. Unemployment is an institution that is 'impoverishing, restricting, baffling, discouraging, and disenabling' (Fryer 1992:114). Specifically, Fryer has shown how unemployment frustrates future orientation, restricts active coping strategies, and restricts through poverty.

In reply to an article by Fryer (1986) Jahoda (1986:27) suggests a one line summary of Fryer's critique: 'he stands for a cognitive social psychology that refrains from systematic analysis of social institutions'. Jahoda argues that Fryer is engaged in a form of psychological reductionism in that he fails to differentiate the social from the psychological dimensions in the functional analysis of unemployment. What this means is that Jahoda is criticised for over-emphasising the institutional dimensions (a sociological reductionism), implying a passive model of the person, and Fryer is in turn criticised for over-emphasising cognitive processes and ignoring the institutional constraints on life (a psychological reductionism).

However, the real problem is not activity versus passivity since most individuals are both active and passive. Individuals shape their lives from the inside-out 'within the possibilities and constraints of social arrangements which we passively accept and which also shape life from the outside-in' (Jahoda 1986:27). Rather, the point is to examine the interplay between social institutions and individual agency. For example, employment commitment and satisfaction with previous quality of employment are both important moderators of the self-evaluative consequences of job loss. They both involve objective and subjective dimensions: actual working conditions and the satisfaction with these conditions; the importance of the work role as part of a person's whole environment, and the subjective centrality of the work role. It is the *interaction* between the objective realities and subjective self-ascription that is critical in explaining the self-evaluative consequences of job loss.

At the end of Fryer's (1986) article he suggests that the attempt be made to develop a more complex, and comprehensive theory including both individual agency and the importance of institutional support. Jahoda (1986), in her reply, accepts this offer of conciliation. Fryer's (1995) subsequent work on the restriction of agency goes some way to developing such a model. However, he retains an undersocialised conception of the person in this work. While Fryer demonstrates that social institutions may restrict people's agency, he does not examine how the goals and activities that are the focus of that agentic action are socially and culturally constructed.

The debate between situation-centred and person-centred models of the individual suggests that any attempt to improve on current theories should incorporate both social and psychological dimensions, recognising the interplay between the person as an active agent, constructing his or her daily life, and the person as constrained and in part determined by social location and social institutions which make up the broader social structure. Fryer himself has made a similar point:

> Unemployed people are agents but their agency is instantiated within complex social institutional contexts: indeed reciprocal aetiological processes operate between individual agency and social institutions. Moreover, both agency and social institutions can each be manifested in both empowering and disempowering forms. (Fryer 1992:265)

Fryer (1992), and Feather (1997), both point out that the failure to adequately theorise the interaction of institutions and agency is a product of the segregation of psychological studies from broader sociological and economic approaches: 'A more inter-disciplinary unemployment and mental health field might be less prone to argue that the mental health consequences of unemployment can be explained in terms of individual agency, relative poverty, social constructed institutions or cultural factors alone and move towards a more considered complex interactionism' (Fryer 1992:265). The approach utilised in this book develops precisely such a 'complex interactionism'.

Job Loss, Status Passage, and Narrative-Identity

Summary of Problems with Existing Research

Existing research into the effects of unemployment tends to be highly descriptive, typically lacking explicit theoretical explanations. Those theories that do exist tend to be overly psychological and rely for their data on self-report, forced response questionnaires. I have identified four main problems with existing theoretical explanations of unemployment.

First, existing theories of unemployment inadequately explain the relationship between objective experiences and their subjective interpretation. More specifically, Jahoda's functional approach and Warr's vitamin model both provide lists of important dimensions of the environments of the employed and unemployed which impact on the social psychological consequences of unemployment. Warr's 'vitamin' theory further provides a well-developed situation centred explanation for some of the variations in the experiences of the unemployed. However, still required is a careful analysis of the variations in the meanings of work and unemployment that takes account of the linkages between objective situations and subjective self-evaluations. Also required is an analysis of the social processes that generate these variations in the meaning of work and unemployment.

Second, the moderating effect of variables such as work commitment, social support, financial strain and the quality of previous work has been clearly demonstrated. However, most theories do not systematically explain the effects of these moderators, lacking an adequate level of complexity and a more general theoretical background to analyse the social psychological processes involved.

Third, most studies of unemployment have not adequately dealt with the temporal aspects of job loss. This is particularly evident when examining the issues associated with transitions from employment through unemployment into early retirement or housekeeping. Static conceptions of unemployment have oversimplified the complex process of negotiation that may be involved in these transitions.

Fourth, some recent studies have examined the role of unemployed people as active agents. However, these studies have not adequately theorised the social and cultural sources of the action they describe.

Finally, while many theories contain an implicit or explicit theory of the meaning of working, this requires further development. An attempt to explain the consequences of unemployment should be clearly related to the sociological and social psychological literature that examines the experience of working.

Existing studies present a complex descriptive picture of the variations in the self-evaluative consequences of unemployment. What is now required is a more careful theoretical explanation of these variations that deals with the interaction between the person and their social environment. To do so it must detail the social psychological mechanisms through which moderating variables have their effect and through which the meaning of working is constructed, thereby incorporating the temporal and negotiated dimensions of job loss.

Theoretical Orientation of Current Study

Unemployment is not a static experience but a process. Unemployment is not merely a status, but one stage within a transition that may involve job loss and re-employment. This transition is also part of an individual's broader biography, including concurrent and past involvements that influence the interpretation of unemployment. More specifically, I suggest that unemployment be reconceptualised as 'job loss' in order to emphasise the processual dimension.

Conceiving unemployment as a process suggests that the important comparisons are not simply between the unemployed and the employed, but between job loss leading into unemployment and other forms of job loss such as retirement, occupational transfer or leaving work to take on a parental role. From a more general perspective, comparisons can also be made with other passages which have similar properties such as divorce, bereavement, serious illness, and the failure of a sporting career.

In other words, job loss is one instance of a more general category of social transitions which Glaser and Strauss (1971) describe as 'status passages'. A status passage entails an individual's 'movement into a different part of a social structure, or a loss or gain of privilege, influence, or power, and a changed identity and sense of self, as well as changed behavior' (Glaser and Strauss 1971:2). To describe job loss as a status passage indicates both the temporal and processual nature of the experience, and the importance of the interaction between objective experiences and their subjective interpretation. More specifically, I use 'status passage' to indicate to the processual nature of the 'objective' events of lived experience and 'narrative-identity' to indicate the temporal nature of 'subjective' self-identity. This point is explained more fully in the next Chapter.

The events of a status passage are interpreted in a narrative, through which a person develops and sustains a self-identity. Drawing on Ricoeur's

(1988; 1992) hermeneutic theory of self-identity as narrative and on interactionist conceptions of the self, I argue that both a remembered past and an imagined future are narratively configured to interpret the events of the present. Conceptualising identity as constructed in a narrative is consistent with McCall and Simmons (1967:202) argument that 'we cannot understand the identities and interactions of a particular moment without considering the influence of relevant life histories'.

The narratives that constitute life histories are not only shaped in response to the events of lived experience, they are also important influences on subsequent actions. Thomas' (1928:584) dictum that 'if people define situations as real, they are real in their consequences' was originally formulated with respect to explaining formative moments during transitional states. Elder (1985:43) succinctly summarises Thomas' argument: 'we cannot neglect the meanings, the suggestions which objects have for the conscious individual, because it is these which determine the individual's behavior'. A narrative conception of identity examines more explicitly the role of remembered pasts and imagined futures in the shaping of self-understandings and choices about how to act.

An examination of the relationship between the events of a job loss passage and their configuration in a narrative focuses on the interaction between a person's objective experiences and their subjective interpretation. Goffman (1976:119) similarly describes the concept of career as 'two-sided' because it allows the analyst to move between the personal and the public sides of the transition processes. It is this interaction between the objective and subjective, between the self and its significant society that forms the dynamic of the narrative interpretation of status passages and transcends the person-situation dichotomy that Warr's situation-centred vitamin model fails to adequately surmount.

While Ricoeur's theory is philosophically sophisticated, interactionist studies have more carefully analysed the social sources of the self, and the structure of the internal dialogue that constitutes the self (Mead 1934; Athens 1994). Interactionist theory has also examined the experiences of embarrassment (Goffman 1967) and shame (Scheff 1991). These indicate the integral relationship between self-evaluations, such as shame or pride, and intersubjective encounters that either sustain or threaten self-understandings. Gergen and Gergen (1988) have further observed that the shape or plot of a narrative is also related to a person's self-evaluations. People may tell tragic narratives about a decline into shame and depression, or romantic narratives the describe a successful struggle to be free from difficult circumstances, resulting in growing pride and confidence. Specifically, the different self-evaluative consequences of job loss can be understood as a product of the different plots that are used to narrate the job loss passage.

The next Chapter develops more fully this theory of narrative-identity and status passage. Following this, the empirical Chapters illustrate how this theoretical orientation can be used to analyse the experience of job loss. Both the events of the job loss passage and the narrative resources that a person brings to their experiences shape the interpretation of the job loss and the subsequent consequences for self-evaluations.

3 A Narrative Theory of Unemployment

Introduction

Becoming unemployed typically changes a person's life story. Different people tell different types of stories. The type of story a person tells about their experiences shapes whether they become depressed as a consequence of becoming unemployed. The story a person tells about becoming unemployed is a complex product of both what happens to them and their skills as a story teller.

The Chapter synthesises three distinct theoretical traditions concerned with the self-concept: Ricoeur's hermeneutic theory of self-identity; symbolic interactionism's analysis of the social sources of the self; and social constructionism's theorising of self-evaluations. Combining the insights of Ricoeur's philosophical analysis with the sociological orientation of the symbolic interactionists and the therapeutic focus of social constructionism provides a subtle, sophisticated, and potent explanation of the changes to self-evaluations associated with job loss.

Narrative theory provides a philosophically sophisticated framework for understanding the self-concept. In *Oneself as Another*, Paul Ricoeur (1992) develops a narrative conception of identity derived from his philosophical hermeneutics. Hermeneutics is 'the critical theory of interpretations' (Rundell 1995:10). In the present context I do not attempt to discuss the philosophical problems addressed by Ricoeur, although some comments will be made at relevant points. The value of Ricoeur's work is that he develops a conceptualisation of narrative-identity that is sufficiently concrete to be empirically useful, particularly when brought into dialogue with symbolic interactionism. However, this conception of self-identity arises out of a thorough and well-articulated philosophical hermeneutics that confronts critically the epistemological and ontological problems raised by the postmodernists (Ezzy 1998a). Ricoeur's approach is explained in greater detail throughout the following Chapter.

Symbolic interactionism examines the social sources of the self. While symbolic interactionism was most influential prior to the 1970s, predominantly in the United States (Strauss 1969; McCall and Simmons 1966; Lindesmith et al. 1977), it has recently been undergoing a revival (Maines 1991; Charmaz 1991; Denzin 1992). Symbolic interactionism

28

identifies the sources of the self in on-going interactive encounters. This focus on the practicalities of interaction emphasises the intersubjective and interactional sources of self-narratives. Interactionism provides a wealth of empirical studies that inform the empirical methodology of the current study, and that furnish important comparative material.

Social constructionism describes the link between self-narratives and self-evaluations or mental health. It refers to a group of predominantly psychological theorists who emphasize the agency of human beings, and who more recently have examined the influence of narratives on human behaviour (Bruner 1986; 1990; Rosenwald and Ochberg 1992; Potter and Wetherell 1987). Social constructionism tends to be oriented toward issues raised in therapeutic encounters (Sarbin and Kitsuse 1994; McNamee and Gergen 1992; Epston and White 1992). Some social constructionists have been specifically concerned with the narrative nature of therapeutic encounters. This conceptualisation provides an explicit analysis of the link between narrative forms and changes in self-evaluations or mental health.

This Chapter argues that understanding identity as a product of the narration of lived experience explains the variations in the self-evaluative consequences of job loss. I begin by arguing for a conceptualisation of identity as a product of the narration of lived experience. Second I explore the implications of this conception of narrative-identity for status passages, particularly those involving the divestment or loss of some aspect of the self. Third I discuss the relationship between narrative-identity and self-evaluations, exploring some recent developments in narrative therapy that suggest changes in self-evaluations can be best explained within the framework of a narrative conception of identity. This leads into an analysis of the relationship between divestment passages, narrative form and self-evaluations. Similar passages can be narrated in quite different ways, and therefore have very different consequences for self-evaluations.

Narrative-Identity

This section explains a theory of narrative-identity. I argue that Ricoeur's conceptualisation of narrative-identity provides a framework for analysing the relationship between the objective events of lived experience and their subjective interpretation. Further, I draw on symbolic interactionist thinking about the self to underline the social sources of narrative identities.

Paul Ricoeur's (1984; 1985; 1988) seminal work *Time and Narrative* examines how people turn historical events into stories. He is not just interested in the structure of the text, as some poststructuralists appear to be. Nor does he ignore subjective interpretation and focus solely on 'objective' events. Rather, his project is *hermeneutic*, in the sense that he is concerned to examine the entire circle in which the events of practical experience are interpreted in narratives, or stories, that in turn shape how people act in the world. Ricoeur's hermeneutics does not begin with the process of interpretation, but with people living in the world. He does not ignore the interpretative process, but neither does he focus solely on it. Ricoeur's hermeneutic analysis 'is concerned with reconstructing the entire arc of operations by which practical experience provides itself with works, authors, and readers' (Ricoeur 1984:53).

Ricoeur's hermeneutics emphasises the reality of lived experience, of acting in the world, as foundational to any attempt to understand the interpretative process. For Ricoeur (1984; 1985; 1988) the text, or narrative, has two 'sides' that interface with lived experience. Lived experience both precedes a narrative, and narrative shapes practical action. The complete hermeneutic circle of narrative and action involves a threefold process of prefiguration, configuration and refiguration. The narrative imagination prefigures lived experience by providing a symbolic structure and temporal schema of action. These events are then configured into a story with a central theme or plot that 'mediates between the individual events or incidents and the story taken as a whole' (Ricoeur 1984:65). This story, or text, then encounters lived experience again in the world of the listener or reader who refigures the story as it influences their choices about how to act in the world.

Emplotment is the process that synthesises experience into a narrative (Ricoeur 1991b:21). Events, which 'just happen', are transformed into episodes that take their place in a unified singular story. Episodes do not just happen, they carry the story along. Events can appear discordant until they are integrated and made sense of in the story. Plot is the organising theme of a narrative. It weaves together a complex set of events into a single story. A plot is not merely imposed, but is produced by a complex moving back and forth between events and plot structure until both are fitted together. Further, emplotment endows the experience of time with meaning. This is the central point of Ricoeur's (1984; 1985; 1988) work *Time and Narrative*.

In volume 3 of *Time and Narrative* (Ricoeur 1988) and in *Oneself as Another* (Ricoeur 1992) Ricoeur uses his analysis of narrative to develop a conception of self-identity. The self, Ricoeur argues, is discovered in its own narrational acts. For Ricoeur, following Heidegger

(1962), selfhood (*ipse*) is ontologically distinct from identity (*idem*). Selfhood refers to the kind of entity that Heidegger (1962) calls *Dasein* and which is characterised by its ability to reflect upon itself. Identity, on the other hand, is a narrative construction that is the product of this reflective process. Narrative-identity constructs a sense of continuity and character in the plot of the story a person tells about him or herself. The story becomes for the person their actual history (Ricoeur 1988:247). G. H. Mead (1934) and the other early interactionists and pragmatists similarly argued that the critical characteristic of the self is reflexivity. Mead's distinction between the 'I' and the 'me' parallels Ricoeur's distinction between selfhood (*ipse*) and identity (*idem*). Mead described the self in terms of an internalised conversation of gestures in which people indicate their self to themselves. 'The "I" is the response of the organism to the attitudes of the others; the "me" is the organized set of attitudes of others which one himself [sic.] assumes' (Mead 1934:175). Ricoeur (1992) takes up a similar emphasis on the importance of others in *Oneself as Another* and this is discussed below.

According to this conception, identities are neither unchangeable substances, nor are they linguistic illusions. The sense of self-continuity in identity is a product of narratives of self-consistency through life's changes. Narrating a life introduces a sense of connectedness and temporal unity to a person's life (Dunne 1995:149). Narratives are integrally temporal because they configure the events of the past, present, and future, into a narrative whole. While narratives can and do change, this does not mean that they cannot provide a sense of self-sameness that is substantial enough to justify talking about, for example, character as 'a persistent unity of preferences, inclinations, and motivations' (Pucci 1992:193). The term 'narrative-identity' as Ricoeur uses it suggests that 'what we call subjectivity is neither an incoherent series of events nor an immutable substantiality, impervious to evolution. This is precisely the sort of identity which narrative composition alone can create through its dynamism' (Ricoeur 1991b:32). Ricoeur captures the middle ground between a sovereign self that is invulnerable and impermeable to the influence of others, and, on the other hand, a deconstructed self that emphasises the linguistic sources of the self and the influence of context 'to the point where it engulfs, if not annihilates, the self' (Dunne 1995:140). The hermeneutics of the self, as Ricoeur (1992:23) puts it, is equidistant from the cogito exalted by Descartes and forfeited by Nietzsche.

Interactionists argued some time ago that the self was not a fixed structure or substance, but a process (Blumer 1969). Similarly, narrative-identities are necessarily processual, or continually in the process of being made, because they describe lived time, which is ongoing. Narrative-identities are very much in-process and unfinished, continuously made and remade as episodes occur. As a consequence, self-narratives often appear confused and chaotic because of the disordered nature of life and because we cannot be sure how the story will end (Carr 1985). This does not mean they do not have a plot, only that it is not simple, clear, or fully worked out. Ricoeur (1984:48) emphasises that plot is not a static structure, but an ongoing integrative process.

The form or plot of a self-narrative is influenced by, and a reflection of, pre-existing narratives from a potentially wide range of sources including myths, movies and past conversations. 'We come to be who we are (however ephemeral, multiple, and changing) by being located or locating ourselves (usually unconsciously) in social narratives rarely of our own making' (Somers 1994:606). Bruner (1987:21) points out that an individual's life story must mesh with the life stories of his or her community in order to be plausible. People are not only constrained by the events of lived experience, but by the limited repertoire of available and sanctioned stories that they can use to interpret their experience. While there are opportunities for identity to be a creative work of style, most people tend to adopt the culturally given plots.

Whether pre-existing narratives, or their sources, are referred to as 'sedimented traditions' (Ricoeur 1985:18), 'public narratives' (Somers 1994), 'cultural repertoires' (Somers and Gibson 1994:73), or stereotypes, these terms all point to the centrality of intersubjectivity and social participation for the creation and maintenance of self-narratives. Self-narratives, therefore, are not the acts of independent individuals, but intersubjective creations of mutual coordination. This leads Bruner (1990:138) to conclude that 'selves are not isolated nuclei of consciousness locked in the head, but are distributed interpersonally'. As Gergen and Gergen (1988:39) put it, each of us is 'knitted into' others' historical constructions, as they are into ours.

Identity is a situational creation, but self-narratives are also historical, held together, as Peter Berger (1966) once said, by the slender thread of memory. The early interactionists explored the relationship between memory and identity in their analyses of the internalised process of role-taking. Reworking their thought provides the basis for a conception of the self that emphasises both its situated and intersubjective nature along with its historical consistency across situations.

Mead's (1934) analysis of taking the role of the other, and Cooley's (1956) concept of the looking glass self can both be seen as exploring the internalisation of the intersubjective process of the creation of self-narratives. The internalised soliloquy (Athens 1994) anticipates and reinterprets through narratives. The self dialogues with phantom, imagined others who inhabit our thoughts and whose perspective we use as we narrate our experiences, past, present and anticipated. It is common to develop new self understandings as issues are 'thought through'. Although nobody else may be physically present, new episodes in our life narrative are recast in the presence of imagined others. To indicate the significance of soliloquies is not to deny the intersubjective nature of the creation of narrative-identity. Soliloquies can be understood as internalised or imagined intersubjective encounters. Further, the importance of internalised others in influencing behaviour explains the historical and enduring aspects of self-presentation. Athens (1994) suggests it is the stability of the phantom others with whom we dialogue that sustains a stable sense of self - and not a Cartesian self substance implied in the thought of Mead and the early interactionists.

Narrated identity provides a sense of personal continuity through time. The narrative integrates lived experience and pre-existing narrative plots in an intersubjective encounter (that may be 'actual' or imagined). A sense of personal continuity, expressed in self-narratives, is grounded in the stability of one's social networks and larger institutions.

Having established a framework for understanding the development and maintenance of a narrative-identity, the next section examines more closely the nature and form of transitions and changes of identity, specifically focusing on the loss of identity. The loss of an identity can be seen as a form of breach that exposes aspects of the self not normally recognised. In the next section I discuss the narrative emplotment of transitions and the symbolic interactionist concept of status passage.

Divestment Passages: Transition and Narrative Plot

Arnold Van Gennep's (1977 [1908]) book on *Rites of Passage* was the first influential exposition of what has come to be called status passage (Glaser and Strauss 1971) (strictly 'rites of passage' refers to the ceremonies associated with 'status passages'). Van Gennep (1977:2) defined rites of passage as 'rites which accompany every change of place, state, social position and age', although he is mainly concerned with life cycle changes such as birth, social puberty, marriage, parenthood and death. As the title of his book suggests, Van Gennep focused on analysis of the 'rites' or ceremonies associated with these transitions: 'for every one of these events there are ceremonies whose essential purpose is to enable the individual to pass from one defined position to another which is equally well defined' (Van Gennep 1977:3).

Glaser and Strauss (1971:2) extend Van Gennep's analysis taking a broader view of status passage as entailing 'movement into a different part of a social structure, or a loss or gain of privilege, influence, or power, and a changed identity and sense of self, as well as changed behavior' (1971:2). They identify a large number of properties of status passages in order to describe the wide variation in modern transitions. Status passages may vary, for example, in the degree of associated ceremony and ritual, the desirability of the passage and the degree to which they are a shared experience.

Van Gennep (1977) originally suggested that rites of passage could be separated into three sub categories: rites of separation, transitional rites, and rites of integration. He also pointed out that some passages focused on integrative aspects, weddings and initiation rites for example, while others emphasised separation, funerals for example. Neither Van Gennep, nor more recent studies of status passages have explored this distinction in any detail. However, I argue that this distinction deserves further elaboration. More specifically, status passages can be divided into two basic types: those that focus on separation and those that focus on integration. In order to distinguish between these two types I suggest that they be referred to as *divestment passages* and *integrative passages* respectively. Divestment passages and integrative passages have quite different properties and consequences for self-evaluations.

Integrative passages usually entail a transitional period followed by integration into a clearly delineated new status entered through a ceremonially specified process. Marriage ceremonies and membership recognition, for example, both focus on celebrating and establishing the person going through the passage in their new identities. On the other hand, *divestment passages* emphasise separation from a status and often contain extended transitional phases of uncertain duration. Divestment passages are, in one sense, negatively achieved. Divorce, becoming sick, job loss and the death of a partner are all typically associated with the failure to successfully maintain or continue in a role. In contrast, marriage, becoming a professional and attaining adulthood are all 'positive' achievements in which a period of growth, training or courtship is successfully negotiated as part of a passage into a new status. Even integration into deviant statuses such as becoming a criminal, or certified insane, involve the acquisition of an identity, rather than simply the loss of publicly acceptable statuses.

This distinction parallels two of the basic narrative modes identified by Northrop Frye (1957) in his *Anatomy of Criticism*: 'In the tragic modes, the hero is isolated from society ... in the comic [and romantic] modes, the hero is reincorporated into society' (Ricoeur 1985:16). Frye's analysis refers to the literary tradition, whereas status passages are lived transitions. Ricoeur argues for the interpenetration of fiction and practical action. This suggests the empirical question: to what extent are divestment passages narrated as tragedies or in other ways? This is one of the issues examined in the following empirical Chapters.

The distinction between divestment passages and integrative passages is not a clear cut dichotomy. Divestment passages are often followed, after a period of time, by integration into a new status and integrative passages are often preceded by, or involve separation from, a previous identity. Whether a particular passage can be classified as a divestment or integrative passage depends on the boundaries of the research and the nature of the actual transition. This is consistent with the point made earlier that lives and narrative-identities are always in-process, and continually developing. Ricoeur makes a similar point in discussing tragedy. The central phenomenon of the tragic action according to Aristotle is 'reversal'. 'In tragedy, reversal turns good fortune into bad, but its direction may be reversed' (Ricoeur 1984:43).

Some examples of status passages that I argue can be classified as divestment passages are illustrated in Table 1. The re-integrative stages are included for completeness, although the focus is on the stages of separation and transition. The question marks indicate that the status into which a person is re-integrated is often uncertain or highly variable.

Table 1 Divestment Passages

Prior Status		Transition		Re-integration
Employed	→	Unemployed	→	Re-employed, Student or ?
Married	→	Separated	→	Single or Re-married
Spouse	→	Widow(er)	→	Single or Re-married
Well	→	Ill	→	Recovered
Athlete	→	Failed Athlete	→	?

Divestment passages are also characterised by an associated normative expectation that the person going through the passage will attempt to move on from the transitional status. The unemployed are expected to search for employment, the sick should try and get well, and the divorced or bereaved should, after an appropriate time of mourning or readjustment, either attempt to re-marry or establish themselves as a 'normal' person. However, such expectations may not necessarily be shared by the person going through the passage or their significant others.

The substantive focus of the current research is the self-evaluative consequences of unemployment. Job loss leading into unemployment is typically a divestment passage rather than an integrative passage. The most commonly associated integrative passage would be unemployment leading into re-employment, although there are a variety of alternative routes out of unemployment. As the experience of the unemployed is the focus of the research, the divestment passage that leads into the unemployed status is of central concern, although associated integrative passages will also be discussed where appropriate.

I use status passage to refer to the more objective aspects of lived experience and narrative to refer to the story about these events. Analysing the events of a passage suggests a less subjective emphasis on lived experience. In contrast, analysing the 'plot' or 'form' of the narrative emphasises the interpretative process through which these events are recast into the episodes of a story. The narrative is not simply a reflection of the events experienced, nor is it only the product of a fictional imagination with no relationship to lived experience. Rather, narrative-identity is the product of the interweaving of the events of lived experience and their subjective significance. Conversely, choices about how to act in particular situations reflect the influence of these narratives. 'The alternation of telling and living is extended in time and ... constitutes a causal chain of sorts' (Rosenwald 1992:273).

Stage accounts of unemployment, discussed in the previous Chapter, attempt to introduce time as an explanatory variable. However, these attempts fail because they simply correlate length of unemployment with self-evaluations. As Ricoeur (1992) has pointed out, it is essential to differentiate objective time from subjective time. Subjective time is the significant factor influencing people's self-evaluations. The subjective passing of time is measured through narrating one's experiences. In other words, temporality is central to the analysis, but not as a simple correlation between objective time and self-evaluations. Rather the temporal succession of objective lived experiences take on subjective significance through the development of a narrative.

Existing sociology typically locates the self in relationships, but not in time (Charmaz 1991:230). Charmaz's analysis of the self in time emphasises the dialectic between events and self understandings. She distinguishes 'time structures' from 'time perspectives' (Charmaz 1991:170). 'Time structures' are the routines, objective structures, and frames of events that correspond to what I have described as the time of lived experience. The concept of 'time perspectives' refers to ideas and beliefs, and the views about the content, structure, and experience of time, and this corresponds to Ricoeur's analysis of 'subjective' narrative time. Charmaz does not explicitly examine the narrative nature of the subjective experience of time, although her analysis deals implicitly with this dimension in various ways. The concept of 'emplotment' developed by Ricoeur theorises explicitly the dialectic between time structures and time perspectives described by Charmaz. 'Time becomes human to the extent that it is articulated through a narrative mode, and narrative attains its full meaning when it becomes a condition of temporal existence' (Ricoeur 1984:52).

Mattingly (1994:811) develops this point in her discussion of therapeutic emplotment. She describes the way in which occupational therapists 'actively struggle to shape therapeutic events into a coherent form organized by a plot'. That is to say, the events of on-going action become meaningful as they are plotted into a coherent narrative structure with a beginning, middle and end. One central feature of the time described in a narrative is that it is different to physical time because 'it is shaped by motive and intention' (Mattingly 1994:817). Mishler (1992:35) similarly describes how the 'strategy of emplotment' enables the person to tell a life story 'as a series of temporally ordered episodes in which transitions can be "explained" as efforts to resolve conflicting motives and pursue certain aims'. Narrative is central to how people understand their life-history. The configurational act of emplotment mediates the historical events of lived time and their subjective interpretation.

A major influence on the temporal aspects of divestment passages are the agents who legitimate and control important stages and transitions. Doctors, for example, often provide estimations of the length of a sickness passage and may legitimate a definition of 'ill' with a medical certificate and also verify a person's recovery. Glaser and Strauss point out that in passages where 'temporal aspects are generally unknown or must be created arbitrarily anew, legitimators and their announcements are of great theoretical significance' (Glaser and Strauss 1971:36). This circumstance is common in the transitional statuses of divestment passages such as unemployment and illness. For example, although Glaser and Strauss intend the idea of recruiting agents to mainly apply to entry into status passages, it is clearly applicable to the unemployed person's attempts to leave the unemployed status. 'In some measure, recruiting may entail the proffering of a passage to the agent or passagee' (Glaser and Strauss 1971:61). Through job applications the unemployed person is continually proffering a passage for re-entry into their occupational career to various agents (employers) who have control over whether their attempt will be successful. Re-employment is the final stage of an unemployment passage.

The lack of certainty concerning the time of leaving the transitional unemployed status has important effects on an individual's ability to control the passage. Oatley and Bolton argue that 'more important than control is the achievement of a degree of predictability that allows mutual plans that satisfy self-definitional goals to be carried through, and that allows a person to build a life of meaning within mutually generated rules and understandings' (Oatley and Bolton 1985:384). The uncertainty of transitional statuses undermines the establishment of routines and committed relationships that would normally provide the basis for a stable sense of self. The effect of this uncertainty increases over time. McCall and Simmons (1966:84) argue that failure to live out role-identities claimed for self leads to the identities becoming increasingly illegitimate in the eyes of self and others. As time progresses it becomes more and more difficult to sustain a role-identity that is not performed.

One mechanism of coping with the uncertainty this situation generates is to relinquish the work identity. In describing the early retirement of retrenched factory workers, Walker and his associates (1984:335) point out that in the status of early retirement 'older workers have at their disposal a socially acceptable alternative role to unemployment, while younger workers do not'. Considerably more social stigma attaches to the status of unemployed than that of early retired, although for some people the hope of re-employment prevented their immediate movement into retirement. This is illustrative of the processual negotiation of a person's response to job loss. Alternative strategies which at first seemed undesirable may, with the exhaustion of more desirable alternatives, become plausible solutions. 'The formal decision to retire prematurely, when it came later [that is after a period of unemployment], was to some extent a rationalisation and an improvement in the individual's situation' (Walker et al. 1984:335).

However, early retirement is only available to the unemployed in a narrow age range. If the work role is central to an individual and a search for employment is unsuccessful over a long period, then the individual may turn to other alternatives that involve a reshuffling of the identity hierarchy so as to reduce investment in the threatened identity or postpone its importance. 'In a sense he [sic.] thus sacrifices a role-identity in an attempt to save the standing of the self as a whole' (McCall and Simmons 1966:101). Examples of alternatives include choosing to return to school or withdrawing from the labour force into a 'housekeeping' role. These strategies return control to the passagee and allow for the development of new alternative identities.

Narratives stretch out in two directions from the present. They both refigure the past and prefigure the future. In terms of narrative-identity people can be seen as setting up life-plans or strategies for interaction in order to maintain the variety of desired role-performances associated with a positive self-narrative (McCall and Simmons 1967:165; Ricoeur 1992:177). Identities require continual legitimation. Strategies or 'life-plans' are designed to provide a stable, dependable source of identity legitimation - typically through the establishment of routines and patterns of interaction with others. For example, the regularity of going to work and interacting with a specified set of others is integral to maintaining a view of self as a 'worker'. Ricoeur argues that life plans also reflect the influence of more general ideals and values. Life-plans are derived from choices about how to apply these ideals and values in practical action.

If there is a major disruption to an individual's life, whether the result of some action of his own or of others, this threatens the whole enterprise of identity legitimation until a 'next best' answer can be worked out to the satisfy the requirements of the variety of desired performances (McCall and Simmons 1966:256). The effects of some divestment passages can therefore be understood as a consequence, in part, of the disruption of strategies designed to sustain consistent and positive self-narratives. I now turn to an explicit analysis of the effects of a devalued identity.

Narrative-Identity and Self-Evaluations

Taylor (1989), Ricoeur (1992), and MacIntyre (1981) have all argued that the self cannot be thought of as a disengaged entity, as a morally neutral ego. That is, they argue the cognitive structure of the self cannot be separated from the moral and evaluative aspects. Narrative-identity is intrinsically evaluative and the self is inextricably a moral entity. Being a self and narrating one's identity involves choices about actions that unavoidably have moral and ethical dimensions. The evaluative dimension of self-narratives is illustrated most clearly in recent developments in narrative therapy (White 1992). Ricoeur (1988:247) observes that in psychoanalysis the very goal of the whole process of the cure 'is to substitute for the bits and pieces of stories that are unintelligible as well as unbearable, a coherent acceptable story, in which the analysand can recognize his or her self-constancy'. Similarly, Polkinghorne (1991:135) argues that 'one function of psychotherapy is to assist in the reconstruction of a meaning-giving narrative of self-identity'. Alternatively, to put this in terms of negative self-evaluations, Polkinghorne (1988:106) suggests that despair and unhappiness can result from either the failure to appropriate the past in narrative or to project a future story.

In *Oneself as Another* Ricoeur (1992) introduces the idea of self-esteem in his discussion of narrative and the good life. 'If self-esteem does indeed drawn [sic.] its initial meaning from the reflexive movement through which the evaluation of certain actions judged to be good are carried back to the author of these actions, this meaning remains abstract as long as it lacks the dialogic structure which is introduced by the reference to others' (Ricoeur 1992:172). That is to say, self-esteem is not arrived at independently of interacting with others. Ricoeur is here making a point about the inseparability of describing and prescribing. A positive description of oneself is inseparable from a prescription for interacting with others in certain ways. This reflects Ricoeur's criticisms of Heidegger's under-emphasis on the importance of others for self-understanding (Kemp 1995), and the influence of Levinas who argued that there is 'no self without another who summons it to responsibility' (Ricoeur 1992:187). In other words, our identity is not found at some deep centre of our personality, rather 'it consists in being recognized by the Others as being the same I and the same person' (Pucci 1992:193). Self-esteem derives from the faithful fulfilment of commitments to others.

The narrative therapists have made a similar point. Gergen and Kaye (1993) suggest that the critical question for therapists is the usefulness of a new story in the contexts that matter for the person outside the therapy situation. In their words, it is not simply any narrative that can be constructed, but the focus needs to be on the 'pragmatics of narrative performance' (Gergen and Kaye 1993:178). 'Change in therapy is the dialogical creation of new narrative, and therefore the opening of opportunity for new agency' (Anderson & Goolishian 1992:28). Negative self-evaluations, therefore, are not simply subjective configurations or stories recounting the past. Negative self-evaluations reflect the inability to plan how to act, with others, in the future (Ricoeur 1992:190). In the interactionist tradition this link between interactional difficulties and embarrassment, shame and depression has been clearly established.

According to Goffman embarrassment is a consequence of threat to or loss of 'face' in interaction. That is to say, when 'the expressive facts at hand threaten or discredit the assumptions a participant finds he [sic.] has projected about his identity' (Goffman 1967:107). Embarrassment occurs in interaction as a result of a problem with self-presentation, the failure to maintain successfully a consistent, shared definition of the situation. Embarrassment is not only part of spoken self-narratives. A person may say nothing at all and yet become embarrassed as a consequence of some action or deed. Embarrassment can also occur when there is no problem with the ongoing interaction, but the imagined responses of others not present leads one of the participants to become embarrassed. How then is embarrassment related to shame?

Scheff (1991), following Cooley and Goffman, identifies shame and pride as primary social emotions that signal the state of a person's social bonds. 'Pride is the sign of an intact bond; shame, a severed or threatened bond' (Scheff 1991:15). Scheff argues that in order to sustain a positive sense of self people require a sense of belonging 'a web of secure social bonds' (Scheff 1991:19). In terms of narrative-identity the failure to narrate an integrated identity that sustains a positive self-evaluation is associated with the disintegration of intersubjective supports for that identity. Shame occurs when a person cannot plausibly narrate a positive self-identity. Soliloquies or internal dialogues with imagined others can also form the basis of a sense of pride or shame. If imagined others are accepting and approving of an imagined activity or presentation, this generates pride. If they are critical or contemptuous, this generates shame and guilt (Scheff 1991:171). Self-evaluations, including pride and shame, are therefore integrally intersubjective.

Not all intersubjective encounters are equally important in shaping self-narratives. Mead (1934) referred to 'significant others' to distinguish those who were more influential on self understandings from those who were not. Similarly, a person's self-narrative can be thought of as hierarchical. If a sociologist demonstrates an ignorance of astronomy, this is not problematic, however if an ignorance is demonstrated of, shall we say, Weber's ideas, this is a potentially shameful and discrediting encounter. Interactionists have traditionally referred to this as identity salience. Identity salience typically refers to a person's subjective evaluation of the importance of an identity to the self as a whole. The salience or centrality of an identity is therefore assessed by reports of self-feeling (Kuhn and McPartland 1954; Turner and Schutte 1981). The idea of a hierarchy of salience applies to a narrative conceptualisation of identity. Narrative-identities vary in their importance, or centrality, to the self as a whole. Some narratives are relatively peripheral, playing a minor role in the construction of self-sameness and coherence. Other narratives are central to a person's sense of identity or sameness. As the structure of a person's activities changes, so do the narratives that sustain a sense of identity. The centrality of a narrative-identity is therefore not fixed, but continually renegotiated. Gergen and Gergen (1988:34) suggest that micro narratives are often nested in macro narratives. People with strong macro narratives can more easily ensure the coherence of their micro narratives.

This nested or hierarchical understanding of self-narratives provides an account of the difference between depression and shame. Depression can be understood as a global form of shame. Shame and particularly embarrassment are typically limited to an interactional encounter, or a small part of a person's social circle. On the other hand, more global negative self-evaluations including depression can be understood as arising when central identities are threatened or lost and there are no alternatives to replace them (Oatley and Bolton 1985:382). Identity is used here in the sense argued for above as a narrative that is maintained and distributed intersubjectively and is dependent on routines. As with embarrassment, it is the discrepancy between the presented self image and the interactional events that is the source of depression. However, the self-image refers to longer term life plans that influence most aspects of a person's self-understanding.

Failure or success in the attempt to sustain a central life plan has a very direct effect on self-evaluations. If people are not successful in finding a social environment conducive to the performance of valued identities and therefore to the development of positive self-evaluations, anxiety and self doubt may result (Turner 1987). Further, if the mismatch between intended strategies and performances is intense or repeated frequently it may lead to psychological disturbance (Thoits 1985; Oatley and Bolton 1985; Goffman 1963:152). According to both Ricoeur and the symbolic interactionist tradition, meaning is not given or inherently present in an object, but emerges through action and in interaction with others. A self-narrative of self-worth is created and maintained through active encounter with the world. When a person is dissociated from established routines and relationships that normally maintain the self-concept, this sense of meaning breaks down, and the person is unable to validate their existence as a 'me'.

However, it is not only the loss of a central role that results in disruptive experiences, but the loss of a central role that is not replaced. Oatley and Bolton make this point succinctly in discussing the causes of depression: 'Our proposal is that the full syndrome of depression that includes loss of the sense of self, dysphoric emotions, and depressive strategies occurs only when a person suffering a role loss is vulnerable in that she or he sees no possibility of an alternative role in which to fulfil self-definitional goals' (Oatley and Bolton 1985:382). The inability to find a replacement for a lost identity is precisely the experience of people who have undergone a divestment passage and remain in a transitional phase, unable to find a satisfactory alternative.

Divestment Passages and Tragic Narratives

Van Gennep also describes the transitional phase of status passages as the 'liminal phase' or 'margin', deriving from the Latin *limen*, signifying 'threshold' (Turner 1969:94). The liminal phase is particularly important in the experience of the unemployed. The unemployed can be seen as stuck in transition, having been separated from their previous employment but still awaiting re-integration into a new job.

A divestment passage leading into a liminal phase has its narrative correlate in the narrative form of tragedies. It is important to differentiate tragedy, which is a well-formed narrative, from testimonies to the ongoing emptiness of the self. Tragedy corresponds to the separation or divestment phase and, in contrast, the ongoing emptiness or meaninglessness of the self corresponds to the liminal phase. Mattingly suggests that social interaction may be more or less narratively configured. At times the plot that is shaped by and shapes action is clear. At other times 'the actors find themselves lost, when there seems to be no point to what they are doing, or when no ending appears desirable, when there is just one damn thing after another' (Mattingly 1994:812).

Ricoeur (1992:248) describes a tragedy as occurring when 'individuals that incarnate spiritual powers and that are brought into inevitable collision by virtue of their one-sidedness have to disappear in death'. Or, as Rasmussen (1995:165) puts it, the dilemma of tragedy is that 'the protagonist appears to be the author or her own activity while spectator and chorus alike know that the narrative itself will eventually overwhelm the character in such a manner that she must succumb to the inevitable unfolding of events'. I will elaborate on the significance of the passivity of the actor in the tragic narrative in later Chapters. Here I want to point out that while a tragedy is a well-formed narrative plot, tragedy leads into an emptiness or absence of plot where events form a meaningless succession. This is illustrated most graphically in one Indian account of the history of the American Great Plains described by Cronon (1992): After the great buffalo herds were gone, nothing happened.

The difficulty of narrating this liminal phase may arise from a number of sources. Langer's (1991) analysis of oral holocaust testimonies points to a vocabulary of disruption, otherness and irreversible loss. The wounded, humiliated and tainted memories of holocaust survivors do not, Langer argues, allow the construction of a narrative with a plot, and they are not tied to time. Langer argues that the events unmake identity, describing an existence without a sense of human agency or moral frameworks that results in a damaged personhood. The experiences of holocaust survivors are an extreme example. However, they point to the disintegrative effects of a set of events that cannot be narrated with a clear plot. A series of events is meaningless until the events become part of a narrative that plots their significance.

The disruption of action is reflected in the disruption of narratives that provide interpretative value. Ricoeur (1992:166) draws a useful parallel with conversion narratives that describe 'moments of extreme destitution'. In these narratives of the dissolution of the self there is an empty response to the question 'Who am I?' However, 'The sentence "I am nothing"' Ricoeur argues 'must be allowed to retain its paradoxical form: "nothing" would no longer mean anything if it were not imputed to an "I". What is still "I" when I say that it is nothing if not precisely a self deprived of assistance from sameness?' That is to say, while the self of being-in-the-world remains, the person is unable to find a narrative to give this self an identity - a narrative of sameness and concordance through time. This correlates with the liminal phase of a status passage where a person is on the margins, or 'in-between', and not clearly in one status or another.

While status passages can be spiritually significant times, as are many of the rites-of-passage analysed by Van Gennep (1977), what is distinctly problematic in modern Western societies is the increasing number of unscheduled, and uncertain passages. That is to say, there are different types of liminality, depending on what is known about the future. Alternatively put, there are different ways of narrating a divestment passage that may or may not leave the person in a liminal limbo. This point is elaborated in greater detail in the following Chapters.

Conclusion

While two people may experience a very similar set of events, they can narrate them in very different ways. Even more pointedly, the same person can narrate the same set of events in very different ways depending on who they are talking to and what they want to emphasise. Riessman (1993:64) argues that not only is it possible to narrate the same events in radically different ways, but that 'telling about complex and troubling events *should vary* because [a story about] the past is a selective reconstruction' (original emphasis). The plot a person uses to narrate their experience reflects how that person perceives and evaluates their life.

I have argued that self-identity is formed in a narrative. While this narrative is shaped by lived experience, it is not determined by it. Narratives give lived experience a clearer and richer meaning. However, self-narratives are not free fictions: 'Humanity, we have said with Marx, only makes its history in circumstances it has not made' (Ricoeur 1988:216). The focus of the study is on the interaction between the events of lived experience and their configuration in narrative. Specifically, the different self-evaluative consequences of job loss can be understood as a product of the different plots that are used to narrate the events of lived experience. These narrative-identities are formed in a complex interaction between events, imagination, significant others, and cultural repertoires.

4 Job Loss as a Romance

Introduction: Three Types of Job Loss

This Chapter and the following three Chapters describe three types of job loss identified from interviews with unemployed people. The three types of job loss narratives are: romances, tragedies, and more complex stories. These types of narratives are distinguished by the structure or plot of the job loss narrative. Figure 1 represents graphically the difference between romances and tragedies. Both begin with positive self-evaluations, but over time these decline. In tragedies, a decline in self-evaluation is initiated by the job loss and a low self-evaluation continues whilst unemployed. However, in the case of romances, self-evaluations declined whilst the person was in their last job. The job loss is a turning point, or moment of reversal, when the person's sense of self-worth begins to improve, and this improvement continues during their period of unemployment. Romance job loss narratives are described in this Chapter. Tragic job loss narratives are described in Chapters Five and Six.

Job Loss as a Romance

Fourteen of the thirty-three people interviewed described their job loss as a clearly positive experience. The form of their narrative is romantic. Their story begins with a regressive decline in self-evaluation, usually expressed in terms of growing frustration, anxiety, and depression. This decline in self-evaluations is viewed as a product of the oppressive and unsatisfactory nature of the interviewee's last job. A turning point comes when a critical event, such as an offer of a redundancy package or the end of a contract, leads to job loss. Job loss is interpreted as a positive event. Unemployment brings both release from an oppressive job, and the freedom to pursue alternative highly valued goals. Although not completely resolved, their problems are diminishing, and they see themselves as justifiably hopeful about their future. There are two types of romantic job loss: strong romances and weak romances. The typical shapes of both forms of romantic narratives are graphically illustrated in Figure 2. This Chapter is divided into two main sections. After describing strong romantic job loss narratives, I turn to consider weak romantic job loss narratives.

Figure 1   The form of tragic and romantic job loss narratives

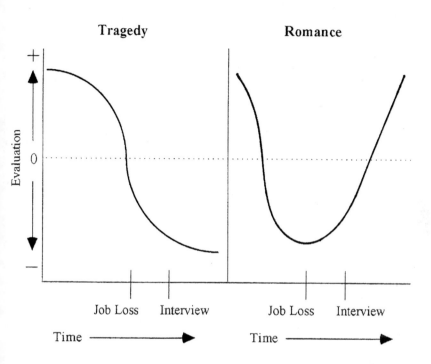

Strong romances give little or no hint of self doubt and provide a clear narrative in which unemployment is regarded as an opportunity to develop, or more correctly redevelop, an alternative career. Current activities support the claim that the future is bright and that the sought after new and satisfying form of employment will soon be found. In strong romances, people describe a clear sense of an alternative career that derives from a story about who they 'really' are. Diana, for example, was 'really' a graphic designer, a claim supported by her university training. She saw her work as a secretary as a hiatus, a discordant event in her path to becoming a graphic designer. I describe this below in more detail as a rediscovery of what individuals considered to be their 'real self'.

Weak romances threaten to become romantic sagas (Gergen and Gergen 1988:26). In weak romances becoming unemployed is portrayed as going on a 'holiday' in one form or another, although interviewees also described themselves as 'unemployed'. While some people wanted their 'holiday' to last as long as possible, various financial, governmental, and social pressures made the story of being on 'holiday' increasingly difficult to sustain. These people were less certain about the future and their experience of unemployment threatened to become dissatisfying in the near future. These romances are weak because being unemployed and 'on holiday' typically only provides a short term alternative to being employed.

Figure 2   The form of romantic job loss narratives

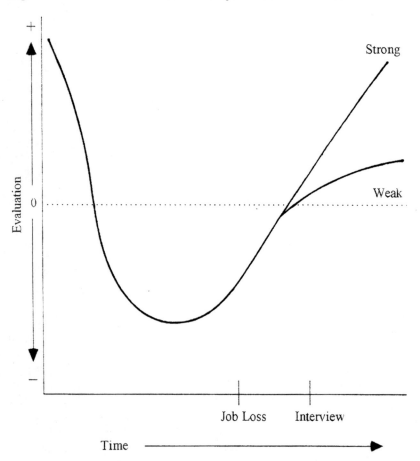

Strong Romances

Five people narrated the events of their job loss as a strong romance. The stories of Geoff and Diana are presented as examples of strong romance job loss narratives. After an overview of their experiences I discuss four themes common to strong romances. First, in strong romance narratives the person rediscovers what they consider to be their 'real self'. They leave an oppressive and morally dubious job to embark on an alternative career in which they can fulfil their 'real self'. Second, these people present a strongly integrated narrative that covers a long time span, reaching back into their educational history and forward into the distant future. Third, the accounts emphasise the agency of the protagonists: people make things happen, rather than passively waiting for things to happen to them. Finally, I discuss the social and financial consequences of job loss that provide an important backdrop that sustains the plausibility of the romantic narratives.

Strong Romances: An Overview

Diana was twenty-six years old when I interviewed her. She held a university degree in graphic design, but had spent the four years since graduation working as a secretary. Diana understood the ending of her last job as an opportunity to take up her career as a graphic designer, or at least as an opportunity to find a job utilising some of her artistic skills. Diana was unambiguously pleased to have finished working as a secretary and described a future that was hopeful, although she was aware of the difficulties she might encounter.

Geoff was twenty-eight years old when I interviewed him, a university graduate in English and Philosophy, living in shared accommodation with no dependants. His last job as a storeman for The Green Organisation lasted approximately two years. Since childhood he had played a number of musical instruments and had continued to play in various rock 'n' roll bands. Geoff saw his job loss as an opportunity to develop a career as a musician. Geoff also was unambiguously certain that leaving his last job was for the better.

There are a number of properties that characterise the leaving experience of Geoff and Diana. Both had at least one month's notice and managed financially without great stress, if not as comfortably as they would have liked. They shared an unambiguous dissatisfaction with their last job, justified on multiple moral and personal grounds, and also had strong friendship networks that were clearly separate from the work environment. They described work as a central part of their lives, although being paid well was not necessarily important. Both characterized the tasks and social environment of the last job as oppressive and dissatisfying. The leaving was portrayed as chosen, and they indicated a high degree of certainty that they would find a more desirable occupation in the future.

The events that formed the basis of their narratives could have been interpreted in other ways. Indeed, similar events were interpreted very differently by other respondents in the study. That is to say none of the properties described above are exclusively associated with romantic job loss narratives. For example, the long notice period was interpreted in one tragic narrative as a time of fear and foreboding during which hope in the future ebbed away.

The properties of the passages are significant because they are the events of lived experience out of which the narrative is constructed. For people like Diana and Geoff, the long notice period provided plenty of time to anticipate and interpret the experience positively. It takes time and energy to narrate an imagined future that is radically different to a person's current activities. Not only did these people have ample notice, they were also well resourced to develop a new and very different future. Diana already had a degree in graphic design and Geoff had been playing music since childhood. Similarly, the strong supportive friendship networks, and absence of major financial pressures allowed these people to continue pursuing a career consistent with what they regarded as their 'real self' when they would have been much more able to easily obtain employment, and money, in a less self expressive occupation.

For Diana and Geoff leaving their job was a planned strategy to develop and explore unfulfilled, and suppressed, skills and talents. This is what made their leaving experience so satisfying, and clearly not distressing. Becoming unemployed was not ideal, it was not an end in itself, but it was clearly a move forward, a step in the direction of self fulfilment. Nostalgia for the past was unthinkable when the future promised so much. There was no reason to be angry or upset about losing their job because they had chosen to leave, it was what they wanted to do.

Geoff and Diana were unemployed for nearly all of the time between their job loss and my interview with them. Geoff was receiving unemployment benefits and Diana had applied for unemployment benefits, but was ineligible due to her partner's high income. Although both had engaged in various forms of part-time and short term casual employment during this period, such employment was relatively rare. It could be argued that Geoff and Diana were not really unemployed because they were not looking for work. However, such an analysis is only half true.

While Geoff and Diana were not looking for work, as a manual labourer or secretary respectively, they were looking for work as a musician and a graphic designer.

Strong Romances: The 'Real Self'

Frye (1957) identified two basic classes or modes of fiction: that of the tragic, and that of the comic. 'In the tragic modes, the hero is isolated from society ... In the comic modes, the hero is reincorporated into society' (Ricoeur 1985:15). Tragedy involves a descent or fall from an ideal state, in comedy the hero ascends to a new ideal state. Romance takes the plot of a comedy and suppresses the funny elements that 'are not really in the plotting but in the treatment of the plotting' (Scholes and Kellog 1966:226). The humour is replaced with 'rich rhetoric' and 'lush description'. In other words, romance is a variation on the plot structure of the comedy.

Romances can be of various types including epic, erotic, and heroic romances. Those described here correspond most closely to the heroic romance depicting the hero in a quest for a distant goal that will eventually be achieved and followed by a return home (Scholes and Kellog 1966:228).

> The Romance is fundamentally a drama of self-identification symbolized by the hero's transcendence of the world of experience, his [sic.] victory over it, and his final liberation from it - the sort of drama associated with the Grail legend or the story of the resurrection of Christ in Christian mythology. (White 1973:8)

While the stories recounted here have the plot structure of a romance, there are some important differences. Scholes and Kellog (1966:236) observe that in modern fiction, the ritualistic - romantic quest for the Grail is metamorphosed 'into the psychological search for identity'. Similarly the romances described in this study describe people's attempts to find an occupation that will both integrate them into society and be consistent with the sense of who they 'really' are.

In the strong romance job loss narratives people describe a clear conception of what they consider to be their 'real self' (Turner 1976) that stands in stark contrast to their last occupation. Geoff saw himself as a musician with a moral conscience and Diana saw herself as a graphic designer who should be using her artistic skills professionally. Both Diana and Geoff's narratives have similar plot structures. Artistic or musical abilities were described as expressed in childhood, their educational career, and other longer term aspects of their personality. Their last job was understood as oppressive and leaving was seen as an opportunity to rediscover their 'real self'. Finding an appropriate occupation is the goal that motivates most of their current actions and sustains a sense of hope that the future can only be better than the past.

When asked to give ten answers to the question 'Who am I?', Diana's initial response was: 'I suppose a very artistic and creative person'. She had attended a very prestigious 'ladies' High School, before completing her degree in graphic design. For Diana, her work as a 'base grade' receptionist seemed inconsistent with her past, and with the occupations of her significant friends. She was embarrassed to tell her friends that she had been working as a receptionist because it had no future, and because it was not utilising her artistic training. She also found it difficult to explain both why she had accepted the position in the first place, and why she had remained within it so long. In short, Diana saw herself as an upper middle class professional or free lance artist. This self conception had its sources in family, schooling, and significant friendships. Her work as a receptionist was presented as a hiatus in her self development. She described herself as now back on course, rediscovering her 'real' self.

Geoff provided an articulate, and well thought through, narrative about leaving a job in order to develop a new career. Geoff had been working for The Green Organisation as a storeman for about 15 months on a casual and part-time basis, before he accepted the position on a full-time basis. In the following extract Geoff describes his change in attitude to working as a storeman:

Geoff: And within about 3 months of full-time work my project was to get enough gear together to be a professional musician and then quit working. And I felt that I'd been duped into working in the first place and I'd sort of lost sight a bit, and I hadn't been working on my novel as much and I hadn't been playing as much and I really missed those things ... I actually did hang around there for about a month longer than I wanted to get the last bit of money together so that I would be able to pay the rego on my car when it became due the next year, because I knew that I would be on the dole and be broke when that came due ... And that's how precise my calculation was of what I wanted to get out of the job in monetary terms, to be able to set myself up as a musician.

Working full-time is portrayed as a hiatus. Geoff felt he had somehow been deceived and had begun to lose sight of the things that really mattered to him. Implicit in the above account is another story that Geoff could have told about how he previously understood his work as a storeman before he came to understand it as oppressive. However, Geoff does not recount this previous understanding that motivated him to stay so long as a storeman at The Green Organisation. To do so would undermine the shape of his narrative that rejects and devalues this last job. The central plot is one of escape from an oppressive and mistaken line of action. Later, when asked more explicitly about why he had been 'duped' into working, Geoff struggled to give an explanation in terms of the influence of a group of friends he had since disassociated from. This group of friends is discussed in more detail below.

The sense of inconsistency between both Diana and Geoff's last occupation and what they saw as their 'real selves' was reinforced with accounts of the immoral and unethical attitudes of the management, and the boring nature and meaninglessness of the tasks. Geoff recounted his growing sense of concern with both the environmental and social justice aspects of some of the activities of his employers: 'The more I was allowed to understand about the way the place worked, the more hypocrisy I saw and the less comfortable I became working there .... I began to feel intensely morally compromised'. Diana found her secretarial work 'boring from the start,' but more importantly in her account, she hated her boss: 'he was a pig, so he was getting worse and worse and more unreasonable'. When twice asked to 'describe the events' leading up to her leaving, Diana did not give an account of events, but rather described how horrible the boss was. This is not surprising due to her extreme dissatisfaction with her work. The stressful work environment had even made it difficult for her to sleep at night. There was no doubt in Diana's account that she had done the right thing by leaving.

Choosing to leave a job required some justification in Australia in the early 1990s. During this period of high unemployment choosing to leave a relatively secure position could easily be seen as irresponsible. In this light it is not surprising that Geoff and Diana gave clear and unchallengeable reasons for their leaving. From their perspective there was no opportunity for regret, and they responded with a clear and unambiguous 'no' when asked if they would like to return to their last job.

Geoff saw himself as a musician and Diana saw herself as a graphic designer. These self conceptions were part of an integrated narrative about their past, present and future. This rediscovery of their 'real self' is like a 'pentimento' (Denzin 1989:81). After having been painted out of the picture of their life for a period, it had re-emerged, and become central. The main problem for Diana and Geoff was explaining why they accepted their last job, and remained in it for so long. However, the portrayal of these acts as misguided or mistaken is a small price to pay for the strength of their current position. The strategy of deprecating or abandoning a threatened or lost identity in order to protect or reaffirm other aspects of one's self was noted some time ago by McCall and Simmons (1966:101). Chiding oneself for ever being concerned with it reduces the significance of that identity. 'In a sense, he [sic.] thus sacrifices a role-identity in an attempt to save the standing of the self as a whole' (McCall and Simmons 1966:101).

Strong Romances: Highly Coherent Narratives

Denzin (1989:62) emphasises the value of establishing how individuals give coherence to their lives. I have argued that coherence lies in the structure of a person's narrative. This coherence however, is not simply rhetorical, it is formed as part of the person's lived experience. Narratives grow out of lived experience and have ongoing implications for acting in the world. Unlike the hopes of some other respondents, both Geoff and Diana had previously been engaged in activities that gave their stories about what might happen in the future a plausibility grounded in the consistency of past, present and future.

The evidence for Geoff's claim that he was 'really' a musician extends both back to his childhood, and forward into a plan for the rest of his life. Further, his plan to become a musician is not merely a pipe dream, but an activity in which he is already engaged:

Geoff: And in the last four months of working [for The Green Organisation] full-time, I'd begun to play bass with The Blues Band, which I considered to be a job. Like, that was a significant job because it was a really good band, really, really high quality standard of music, really exciting emotionally and musically really demanding and so much fun to play and I was pulling minimum every week 140 bucks cash in hand, which was the dole ... And that was what I'd been wanting to do. And because of that, because of playing in The Blues Band, I started, the other peripheral things that I'd felt like I'd been wasting my time with the last few years, started to drop out of my sight as goals. I started to think, 'yeah I am a musician, my first impulse on leaving school was right, I should be trying to make a living as a musician. This is what I'm best at, it's what I enjoy, it's the job that fits me exactly. This is what I want to survive doing for the rest of my life'. And so I quit work. My time with The Blues Band finished around about the time I quit work, unfortunately, because it was just a part-time thing until their original bass player came back, which he did.

Again Geoff alludes to, but does not detail, a former way of understanding his work as a storeman that he now rejects. 'Other peripheral things' started to lose their importance because of his work in The Blues

Band. The phrase 'I started to think' indicates that this process of reorienting his priorities and self-understanding had begun months before he finally left his job. Further, as discussed below, this process continued into his experience of unemployment.

Diana describes a similar current concrete affirmation that her skills were marketable and could in the near future lead to a full-time occupation. Diana had applied for jobs as a graphic designer, and having been interviewed on most occasions anticipated that it was probable she would be offered a job 'working for someone else' at some stage soon. At the same time, she was also considering 'starting up my own business' and was taking steps to officially register her own design. Diana was confident that this venture had a reasonable chance of success because she had recently sold some of her artwork in local stores and at a local market. In short, there was little doubt in Diana's account that she would soon be employed in some way that was consistent with her skills and sense of self as an artist.

Geoff and Diana's career aspirations involved them in an active effort that, if only rewarded sporadically at present, promised to lead in the near future into a full-time occupation. Geoff and Diana's plans were clearly different to those of other unemployed people because Geoff and Diana were engaged in activities whilst unemployed that supported the plausibility of their plans. Further, the difficulties of succeeding in their new career and of a period of unemployment were anticipated. Geoff saved for the registration on his car due in six months time. Diana had arranged to attend a course on computer skills in graphic design immediately after leaving her job. Not only was the alternative career imagined, but concrete actions required to reach that alternative had been considered and incorporated into their current activities.

These career oriented activities transformed the experience of unemployment. Being unemployed was desired, and therefore not frustrating. Rather, unemployment provided freedom from an oppressive occupation and an opportunity to work toward a new career. The goal of a new, more satisfying career provided the focal point for a full and busy lifestyle. It is this active engagement that makes their experience of unemployment positive and valued.

Strong Romances: Agency

Riessman (1990:1197) observes that climactic points in narratives are typically dramatised. This can be seen in the job loss narratives collected in this study. In Geoff's narrative he dramatises his thoughts on two occasions, both of which emphasise that leaving his last job was an intentional choice:

Geoff: I started to think, 'yeah I am a musician, my first impulse on leaving school was right. This is what I want to survive doing for the rest of my life'. And so I quit work.

Whether or not a person actually chose to leave is less important than the ability to portray the leaving as consistent with a line of action that was desirable. This meant that they were able to portray themselves as 'in control' of their lives. In contrast tragic narratives, discussed in the next Chapter, typically describe people as pushed around by fate and unable to control their lives, even when they describe the ending of their last job as partly, or entirely, the result of their own choice. Mike's experience demonstrates this point clearly. Mike was thirty-two when I interviewed him. His last occupation as an architect had ended nearly a year before and, like Diana and Geoff, the form of his narrative is a strong romance. His account illustrates the difficulty of defining a leaving as either forced or chosen. In Mike's case this ambiguity turns on the difference between being forced to leave his job, and choosing to use being unemployed as an opportunity to change his vocation. Mike uses this ambiguity strategically to silence some of his family who would otherwise have criticised his decision to stop working as an architect:

Doug: It seems your family weren't happy?
Mike: No, but at the same time, leaving work wasn't a decision, it may have been something I was going to do, but as it turned out it wasn't. So there was a beautiful inevitability about it that kept the parents from asking too many pointed questions. Because, I had been sacked, effectively. It was the fault of the recession and society at large, rather than a personal decision that I had made.

In one sense Mike had no choice about his sacking, and this is the version of the story he presents to his parents. However, Mike suggests that 'really' he did have a choice, because it was something he was going to do anyway. In other words, Mike is able to portray himself as in control of the situation and it is this sense of autonomy and control that supports his sense of purpose and self-worth, even though he is unemployed. A similar relationship is noted by Charmaz (1991:259) in her account of people dealing with chronic illness. People retain a sense of self-respect if they are able to retain a sense of autonomy. When a person believes that they can still make autonomous choices despite significantly diminished options this enables them to preserve their sense of self-respect.

One participant became angry when I asked her a couple of times about the reactions of other people to various events she was describing, denying that they were important. This tendency to deny other people's influence on the decision making process appears to be associated with a sense of being autonomous and in control. Mike's response to a question about his friends makes this point clearly:

Doug: What did some of your more important friends think about you leaving work?
Mike: You would have to ask them Doug [laughs].
Doug: OK, what do you think some of your more important friends thought about you leaving?
Mike: I don't think they had any problems with it, if that's what you mean. It also depends how susceptible you are to your friends and sort of peer group stuff.
Doug: How susceptible are you?
Mike: Bugger all [laughs]. Very little.

The decision, Mike emphasises, was not influenced by others, but was his own choice. Leaving the last job is portrayed as an intentional strategy, where the person takes control of their life. Friends' opinions may feature in the account, but this is usually in terms of either condemning the inappropriateness of the last job, or as passive supporters of the transition. Friends, or other people, are not significant actors in these stories. The discovery of one's 'real self' is described as a deeply personal and individualistic experience that is explained in terms that emphasise the person's control over their own life. When other people are described as influential, they are mainly negative influences. For example, they deceive the person into inappropriate jobs, or do not understand the real importance of what the person is doing, and are dismissed. Similarly, people who left a job in order to have a holiday did not describe themselves as forced into this situation by the actions of others. Rather, their narratives appear designed to demonstrate that their experiences and actions are the consequences of their own choices. This individualistic and autonomous view of the self elides, or ignores the social processes through which the self is constructed (Ezzy 2000). The importance of being able to impute agency to oneself in narrative accounts of one's actions will become clearer in the Chapter on tragic narratives.

Strong Romances: Social Support and Financial Survival

In Chapter Three I argued that self-narratives are not acts of independent individuals, but intersubjective creations of mutual coordination. An individual's life stories must mesh with the life stories of his or her community in order to be plausible. The importance of other people to the creation and maintenance of narrated identities is clear in the responses to friends who both affirmed and rejected explanations of job loss.

When people were comfortable talking about the attitudes of their friends (and this was not always the case) they typically described positive responses. Diana, for example, described her friends as supportive:

Doug: And how did [your friends] respond to you leaving your job, what did they think?
Diana: They think it's good. They said 'oh you should use your skills'.

The responses of Diana's friends are generally supportive, and affirm the detail of Diana's explanation for leaving her last job. Diana described her current status as 'unemployed,' or rather, an artist beginning her career, as more acceptable to her upper middle class friends than her previous occupation as a 'base grade receptionist'.

However, not all friends were supportive of interviewees' explanations of their job loss. One way of dealing with disapproving friends was to disassociate from them. Geoff successfully employs this strategy because he also had strong ongoing associations with approving friends that replaced the lost relationships. The disapproving circle of friends saw Geoff's job as a storeman as appropriate for Geoff. Geoff both relinquished his job as a storeman and disassociated himself from these friends who could not understand his decision. A different group of friends, predominantly musicians, were very supportive of Geoff's decision to embark on a musical career. Geoff, therefore, did not feel isolated and was able to find sufficient social support for him to believe his decision was correct.

The absence of financial distress was also an important foundation of Geoff and Diana's narratives. While Geoff and Diana would prefer more money, financial concerns were not described as highly distressing. Geoff had lived below the poverty line for some time, had no debts and had learnt to survive bearably, if not comfortably on unemployment benefits. Diana was supported by her working partner and while money was 'tight', they were 'managing'. Having sufficient money is important for sustaining both routine activities and social relationships (Simmel 1990:313, 326). The important point for Diana and Geoff is that while they would like more money, their financial situation whilst unemployed was sufficient to sustain their routines and friendships. Their romantic narrative that includes a sense of improved well-being in the present and a clear hope in the future is consistent with their current financial situation.

Strong Romances: Self Esteem

That a group of people did not find unemployment distressing is not surprising. This has been previously documented in the unemployment literature (Fryer and Payne 1984; Jahoda 1984; Fryer 1986). However, I want to emphasise the source of this positive experience of unemployment. It is not simply that these people were engaged in activities that performed the same functions as being employed, as Fryer and Jahoda suggest. I argue that the plot of the story cannot be separated from their experiences, and that this relationship between the events of the job loss passage and their interpretation in a narrative is the critical influence on self-esteem.

The plot of the narratives described here were not clearly determined by the events of the passages. However, historical events together with the support of friends, a clear self-concept, and an imagined future enable the construction of a romantic narrative. Romantic narratives emphasise choice and control over decisions. They are clearly coherent on a number of dimensions. The narratives integrate a long biographical time period in which each of the episodes warrants or supports the general theme of the story that the person is 'really' a musician or artist. The episodes in the narrative are also consistent with motives, actions, and feelings (Rosenwald 1992:285). Finally, the coherence of the narrative is a cooperative achievement in the sense that close friends are supportive of interviewee's interpretation of events (Linde 1993:12). The narratives are romantic because they represent an attempt to overcome an otherwise difficult experience through a heroic search for a new, or renewed, identity. It is the ability to narrate a story with this form or plot that sustains Geoff and Diana's positive self-evaluations whilst unemployed.

Weak Romance Narratives: Unemployment as a Holiday

A second group of people also described their job loss in positive terms. They too were pleased to finish their last job and looked forward to being without work. Rather than seeing job loss as an opportunity for a career change, they looked forward to unemployment as an opportunity to relax and enjoy themselves, to have a holiday. Similar to the rediscovery of one's real self, leaving a job to go on holiday has the plot structure of a romance. The story begins with the oppressive nature of the last occupation. A turning point leads to the person's release into a highly desirable period of freedom, a 'holiday'. During this period self esteem is high. However, this golden period is short lived, and the narrative threatens to turn into a romantic saga or a tragedy. At the time of the interview the positive aspects of being on holiday were either on the wane, or threatened to do so in the near future. For this reason I refer to the plot of these narratives as weak romances.

People who narrated their experience as a weak romance tended to describe work as less important than other people in the study. Work was described as dissatisfying, oppressive, or unpleasant in some way, although these feelings were based on situational rather than strong moral arguments. Unemployment was not regarded as financially distressing, although some people only felt financially secure for a short time, typically less than a year. Even if the formal notice period was short, job loss was anticipated and desired. As with the strong romance narratives, people described their job loss as consistent with their desires, even if they were forcibly retrenched.

These properties provide the foundations for the plot of the job loss narrative. Dissatisfaction with the last job supports an interpretation of job loss as a release that brings freedom. The absence of financial pressures allows the person to sustain their claim to be on holiday, albeit for a limited time. The lesser importance of work is consistent with the claim that the absence of paid employment resulted in an improved life. Short term financial security and increasing dissatisfaction with being unemployed meant that the claim to be on holiday could only be sustained for a short time. High self esteem was sustained while the claim to be 'on holiday' remained a plausible explanation of what the person was doing. Self esteem declined and depression and anxiety threatened to develop as the claim to be on holiday became increasingly inconsistent with the person's activities.

Of the nine accounts in this group I will draw examples from the experiences of Joyce, a kindergarten teacher, Bill, a landscape gardener's labourer, and Ruth, an electronics technician. According to some definitions some of these people do not qualify as 'unemployed'. Joyce, for example, left for a three month trip around the world after finishing her job, and Ruth initially had little intention of seriously looking for work. However, Ruth was receiving unemployment benefits, and Joyce's overseas trip was as much a face saving strategy as it was desired for its own sake. Joyce looked for work both before and immediately after her trip, and on her return was eligible to apply for unemployment benefits, although she chose not to apply. In other words, it is too simple to define people who describe themselves as on holiday as not unemployed. While in some cases the transition from being on holiday to unemployment is clear, in other cases the experiences overlap to such a degree that it is difficult to separate them.

Ambivalent attitudes toward work and unemployment feature prominently in these accounts. The reasons for making choices are not as clear as in the strong romances, and the narratives are therefore not as internally coherent. People report mixed feelings about their last job. Ruth enjoyed her work as an electronics technician, and the friendships of her work associates. However, she found the management unbearable, and felt her future in the company to be uncertain. Joyce identified a wide range of problems with her job, but still valued it enough to be prepared to consider continuing there if a position had been available. These ambivalences are parallelled by ambivalent attitudes toward unemployment. Unemployment is initially celebrated, and continues to be seen as mostly a positive experience. However, over time, unemployment becomes increasingly problematic and potentially distressing. Ambivalence also characterises attitudes toward friends. Bill, for example, both envied the lifestyle of unemployed friends and avoided them because he found their attitudes 'negative'.

Weak Romances: A Holiday as a Reason for Wanting to Finish Work

In weak romances people explained their leaving in terms that were not as forceful and morally compelling as the strong romance narratives. However, they did not regret leaving. There was no sense of embarrassment at having worked in their last job and the reasons for leaving were not bound up with a strong desire to pursue a very different career. If this group of people were now offered work in a job similar to the one they left, they would be likely to consider the offer. This stands in contrast to Geoff and Diana who would definitely refuse such an offer.

Bill was thirty-eight when I interviewed him, and lived by himself in a rented flat. He had been unemployed for nearly a year. Bill was sacked from his last job with a few hours notice. Although he had no control over his dismissal, it was something that could be described as desired:

Bill: When I got laid off it was out of my hands. But I had done that [job] for nearly two years and I was hoping that something would happen because we'd all had enough of it ... Then when [the boss] came up to us and said

'sorry, Bill, I'm going to have to lay you off', I said 'oh yeah', and I tried
to keep the smile off my face and I said 'oh that's really, [pause] no worries
Kev', I said 'I can understand that completely'. And as I walked away I
said 'yippee'. So I was happy then to get out of it.

Doug: Why were you happy to get out of that?

Bill: Oh it was just so hard to drag myself out of bed at six every morning to
start at seven and work through two winters, digging in the rain and
working in the rain, the same thing every day and just, I guess it was
monotonous, getting to that point where the joy had gone out of it.

Even though Bill was sacked, it was something that he wanted and
had been contemplating for some months. Lived experience facilitated
and supported Bill's hopes and desires, rather than working against them.
It is impossible to tell if Bill 'really' wanted to leave his job at the time
he was sacked or whether he felt differently at that time. However, for
the purposes of this discussion, it does not matter. The point is that
Bill, in retelling his job loss, constructs it as a positive experience by
describing the ending as desirable and anticipated. To identify oneself as
desiring a holiday is one way of narrating the past so that desires and
events are consistent.

The reason Bill gives for wanting to leave is not morally compelling.
He was bored and hoping for a change. He did not feel strongly enough
to leave himself, but was pleased to be sacked. Bill also presented his
last job, and the experience of becoming unemployed as continuous with
his past. He had been unemployed a number of times for various periods,
and this latest experience was, if anything, easier because he knew what
had to be done. Although hoping for something different in the future,
he anticipated he would be doing the same low paid manual work for the
rest of his life.

Joyce's job loss illustrates the complexity of trying to identify whether
or not some people choose to leave. Joyce was 55 when I interviewed
her, living in her own home with one of her three children. Three
months before the end of the year she was told that her contract as a
kindergarten teacher would not be renewed the following year. While
she knew that some people were leaving, which meant there was a good
chance that a job would still exist for her, Joyce decided to leave anyway,
telling her supervisor that she did not want to work there the following
year:

Joyce: So as I'm driving home I thought 'what a fool, you have given away a job'
and then I thought 'no'. Emotionally I didn't have the energy left to do
what I wanted to do and my first priority was to work on my relationship
with Alex [her partner] ... And I thought 'what I need is a face-saver'. I'd

been talking about going to see Bruce [her brother who lived overseas] for 10 years, 'right, I'm going'. So I made up my mind like that.

Both Joyce and Bill dramatise the event of leaving. In both narratives this dramatisation emphasises their choice and control over the situation. Even though they may not have been able to choose to stay at work if they had wanted to, they present their leaving as an active decision to go on holiday. It is this reconciliation of narrative-identity and the events of lived experience that enables them to sustain their positive evaluation of the experience.

Doug: Compare how you feel now with how you felt about the middle of last year. Do you feel better or worse?
Joyce: Everybody, including, I spoke to John [a work associate] today ... [and he said] 'Oh you look wonderful', and that's how I feel. I don't feel anywhere near as physically stressed.

Bill said 'Yippee' when told of his sacking. Further, although he found unemployment a difficult experience previously, this time: 'I've really enjoyed the rest ... It's all right for a while, but I wouldn't want to be doing it, hopefully, for the rest of my life'.

To be on holiday is a socially valued and positive role. It provides a line of action that is typically short term, but that gives an explanation for the leaving that enables the speaker to retain an image of themselves as in control of their lives. In Joyce's case, going on holiday was the public justification that also made her decision to leave simple and clear. At various stages of her account Joyce gave a number of much more subtle and complex reasons for leaving: she was feeling too old and tired to continue in that occupation, she disliked the management and there were problems with adequate resources to do the job well, she wanted to devote energy to family relationships, some of her clients had given her a hard time, and her job may not actually have been there the following year. However, Joyce also said: 'I think if I'd been offered a job I would have gone back'.

This comment points to the much more ambivalent relationship these people had to their last job. While there were good reasons for leaving there were occasional indications of regret and yearning for things such as lost friendships, status, and security. While describing their last job as unpleasant allowed desires and events to be presented as consistent, this line did not cover all the described feelings about their former position, some of which were still clearly positive. This tension and inconsistency in their stories about leaving in order to take a holiday becomes more evident in the accounts of how they felt once they were actually without work.

Weak Romances: The Short Term Nature of Holidays

Bill described the beginning of his 'holiday' as an unemployed person as deserved and enjoyable:

Bill: But I did find that there was just no time to do anything [while I was working]. And then a lot of my friends would lose their jobs or whatever, so they wouldn't be working either. And they seemed to be having a good time and I'd always have to say 'look I have to go home now'. And I found that, I felt that I was just missing out on a lot of things ... So not working meant that I could visit people, go shopping, do the things that I wanted to do. You'd go for walks in the park, you could read, spend lots of time doing that sort of stuff ... It's nice, you can get up at 10, you can go to bed at 12, you watch all the late-night movies, you can do whatever you want. It's nice, it's like being on holiday. But then, after a while you realise 'oh well, this is it'.

While Bill described unemployment as initially pleasurable, this pleasure did not continue. A little later in the interview he recounted a growing ambivalence toward the lifestyle shared by his friends who were also mostly unemployed and part of a well-organized cafe culture that he found both enviable and to be avoided:

Bill: At first it was OK, you know, going visiting them in the daytime and so forth and hanging round together and doing things together, but now I'm finding that after about 6 months, that that's now got to the point where I'm thinking, well I need to do something for myself. Because if I just hang around with these people, I then adopt their lifestyle and it's coffee in Main Street, tea and coffee every day, it's that sort of thing. And then you start thinking, and if they're negative as well about, [pause] sometimes you can just breed negativity, you know. You hear about the unemployed figures, 'yeah, no bloody hope of getting a job, oh yeah' [pause]. So I sort of left their thinking. 'No I'm not, I want to keep positive, no, I've got to' [pause]. So I've pulled away from a lot of those day time meetings with people who are unemployed otherwise you just become a little sub-culture and then you start to accept that this is the way life is going to be.

On the one hand, Bill appeared to want to reject the lifestyle and 'negative' rhetoric of his unemployed friends who were not looking for work. On the other hand, he clearly found this world attractive because it allowed him to accept his unemployment, and enjoy it as a holiday.

Being on holiday had become increasingly dissatisfying for Bill because it did not provide him with enough structured activities and a sense of worth as a worker. Joyce also found the lack of structure and social stimulation distressing. This was exacerbated by a growing concern about the financial consequences of being unemployed. All these problems work together to make the experience of unemployment increasingly distressing with the passage of time.

Justifying leaving a job on the grounds of having a holiday does not typically provide a long term plan. There are some long term unemployed people for whom unemployment has become an open ended holiday (Bakke 1934; Turner et al. 1984). No-one in this sample fitted this description. Some people only intended to be 'on holiday' for a specified period of time, and then began to describe themselves as unemployed. Others attempted to sustain the claim to be 'on holiday' for extended periods. However, with the passage of time, diminishing resources, and the end of planned activities, the claim to be 'on holiday' became difficult to sustain. This led, in varying degrees, to increasing anxiety, restlessness, boredom, loneliness and the desire to again find work. In short, being 'on holiday' was typically successful only as a short term strategy that supported a positive interpretation of the job loss event.

Weak Romances: Friends and Finances

A person without paid work who describes themselves as 'on holiday' presents an image of their life as under control. They are doing what they want to do. Lived experience and desires are consistent. This strategy for saving face, for presenting an 'internally consistent line' (Goffman 1967:6), was not equally successful or sustainable. The closer a person's actions were to what is typically thought of as a holiday, the more successful and acceptable this 'line' was for the period of the 'holiday'. Joyce went overseas to visit her brother, following almost exactly the pattern of a traditional holiday. Bill, on the other hand, did not go anywhere and was drawing unemployment benefits. As a consequence, Bill's feelings of being on holiday were much more short lived than Joyce's. Joyce encountered hardly any resistance from her friends. On the other hand, Bill encountered a significant negative response from some of his friends.

When asked what her more important friends thought about her decision to leave work and go overseas Joyce said: 'Alex said "wonderful idea" he said "go for it". Paul said "I was saying to Joanne, we must get Mum to go overseas"'. Joyce could only think of one person who had disapproved, and his concerns were mainly about finances. Her description of these responses also suggests that her holiday narrative was an act of mutual coordination.

The clearest account of the significance of disapproving friends was given by Ruth. Ruth was thirty-three years old when I interviewed her and had been unemployed for nearly a year. She lived alone in an inner city flat that she owned. Her last job was with a large electronics firm who had employed her for seven years as an electronics technician and trainee manager. While some of Ruth's friends were not worried by her unemployment, most notably her tennis partner, others were less sympathetic:

Doug: What about your [other] friends outside work, what did they think about you leaving?
Ruth: They weren't impressed.
Doug: Why not?
Ruth: I don't know, most people, especially Jews, there's this emphasis on for starters you only hang around with people who are successful and that makes you successful, there's this theory. Plus, people can't handle the fact that you don't want to work. I don't know what's wrong with them. A lot of people don't like it. I don't know why.
Doug: So how did you feel about that?
Ruth: Oh, I wasn't impressed about that either, I thought: 'Get lost'. Well, because, you know, it's my decision. It's my life. And I'm not asking anyone for anything. So what's the problem?

Ruth refuses to grant any plausibility to those who criticise her decision to leave. She begins and ends her response disclaiming any knowledge of why these people might be critical of her. Ruth argues that she is 'not asking anyone for anything'. However, she is receiving unemployment benefits. This indicates the contradictory character of Ruth's story. She claims to be on holiday, when she is, at least officially, also claiming she is unemployed and looking for work. There were a small number of people prepared to join Ruth in her 'holiday' activities without questioning her status as 'unemployed', but even these people had begun to move on or see less of Ruth. As a consequence, she was feeling increasingly isolated, and under pressure from her remaining friends to give up her claim to be on 'holiday'.

People who described themselves as 'on holiday' were typically not financially stressed. Bill was the poorest, with few savings that had been spent early in his unemployment. However, while he would prefer more money, he was well adapted to living on unemployment benefits. Joyce also had some savings, although only sufficient to provide for a limited number of months. Ruth received a large redundancy payment, owned her flat and was financially secure for the long term, particularly if she continued receiving unemployment benefits. In other words, to describe oneself as being 'on holiday' minimally requires that the person can sustain themselves financially. However, all the respondents in this category described themselves as increasingly under financial pressure and becoming more dissatisfied with the constraint on spending that being without work imposed on them.

Conclusion

This Chapter has described two types of job loss associated with improved self-evaluations: strong and weak romance job loss narratives. I have argued that it is the structure of the narratives that sustains these positive self-evaluations. Narratives are developed out of the passage of lived experience, and this passage must have certain properties for the narrative to be plausible. Narratives are also not developed in isolation. The support of significant others is required to sustain an understanding of job loss as either a regaining of one's real self, or as a 'holiday'. While the structure of these narratives is that of a romance, some threaten to become tragedies. The next Chapter examines narratives that have the plot structure of a tragedy.

5 Job Loss as a Tragedy

Introduction

To be unemployed is to be, by definition, not something that a person should be. At the heart of the trauma and depression experienced by the unemployed people discussed in this and the next Chapter is the inconsistency between their status as an *un*-employed person and their desire to be employed. Tragic job loss stories describe this experience painfully and unerringly. The dream of what might have been between the two lovers in Romeo and Juliet stands in stark contrast to their deaths. Similarly, the story about what might have been if the good job had continued stands in stark contrast to the often brutal experience of being without employment.

Tragic narratives have two distinct phases that correspond to Van Gennep's (1977) stages of separation and transition. First, people describe the trauma of losing their job. The focus of this trauma is the loss of certainty about the future that secure employment provides. The way in which a person is retrenched is the main source of variation in the way people respond to losing their job. Second, people describe the trauma of being unemployed that focuses on the struggle to find work. A sense of being unwanted and worthless because a person is unable to find work leads into periods of depression and self-deprecation. However, some unemployed people also described more constructive times of active job search and a stronger sense of self-worth.

This Chapter focuses on the experience of tragic job loss, while the next Chapter discusses the experience of tragic unemployment. Unlike romantic job loss narratives, in tragic narratives the experience of job loss is clearly differentiated from the experience of unemployment. Whilst the way a person is retrenched may affect their experiences at the time of their job loss, in tragic narratives the effects are typically short lived. For these people the experience of unemployment is influenced by factors unrelated to the type of retrenchment.

In tragic fiction 'the hero is isolated from society' (Ricoeur 1985:15). Tragic job loss narratives describe a similar process in which the person becomes separated from society. These accounts typically describe a person whose sense of being part of society is integrally entwined with their self-identity as a worker. Job loss destablizes this self-identity and undermines the person's sense of their place in society. Job loss is a tragedy because both the loss of employment and the consequent period of unemployment are harrowing experiences that result in feelings of isolation and worthlessness.

This Chapter begins with a discussion of the central characteristic of tragic narratives: the undermining of an imagined and desired life plan. The ruining of a life plan leaves the unemployed person in a liminal, or in-between, state in which they fear an ongoing exclusion from society. The depression and anxiety experienced as a consequence of job loss derive from the tension between desired life plans and the anticipated experience of being unemployed. This tension or inconsistency is central to tragic job loss narratives. Four variations on the basic tragic form are identified and discussed in the remainder of the Chapter: traumatic tragedies, moderated tragedies, ironic tragedies and sustained tragedies.

Tragic Job Loss: A Ruined Future and a Devalued Self

Of the thirty-eight job loss narratives examined, twenty-four are tragic in form. The main characteristic of the tragic narrative is a sharp decline in self-evaluations as a consequence of the job loss event and this is represented graphically in Figure 3. The tragic nature of the experience derives from the inconsistency between the status of being unemployed and an imagined and desired identity of 'worker'. It is this inconsistency that is the source of the distress and anxiety experienced as a consequence of being retrenched. Rosenberg has made a similar point:

> In sum, it is plain that we can never attain an adequate grasp of the self-concept without taking account of man's [sic.] extraordinary tendency to visualize himself as other than what he is, to construct in imagination a picture of what he wishes to be. No one can see himself as bad or good, admirable or contemptible, except with reference to the standards he has set for himself. (Rosenberg 1979:45)

This gap between the reality of lived experience and an imagined and idealized standard against which a person compares him or herself is at the heart of tragic job loss. Rosenberg's analysis needs to be extended to take into account the narrative and temporal nature of the self-concept. The comparison is not simply between an extant self-concept in the present and an idealized self-concept in the present. Comparisons are also made between stories about a likely future as an unemployed person and stories about what a person had been in the past and could achieve in the future if they were securely employed. Specifically, the main source of distress associated with tragic job loss is a consequence of the discrepancy between an imagined, and feared, future of unemployment and an imagined, and desired, future as a worker.

Figure 3   The basic form of tragic job loss narratives

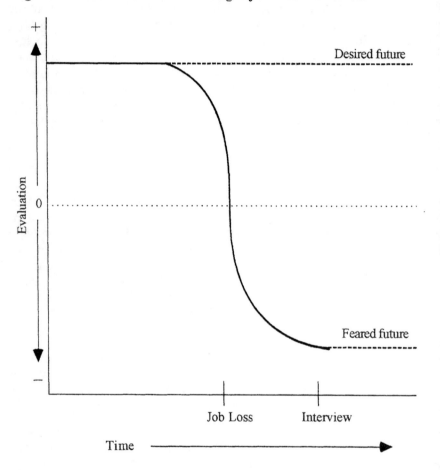

Lyn was twenty-six years old when I interviewed her. She las worked eight months prior to the interview as a secretary for a smal business. Lyn captures clearly the inconsistency between her desirec future as a worker, and the anticipated experience of unemployment:

Lyn: It is rather depressing actually. I just thought 'where am I going', I jus thought, 'what am I doing with my life?' Like, I think some people know have got jobs and are working and I just think it's not fair ... And just felt I really want to get a job and I really want to do something with myself and have a future.

Narrative-identities reach back into the past and forward into the future. Stories about what a person has done in the past provide a sense of continuity and integration that sustains a person's sense of self-identity. Life plans, or strategies for interaction, are stories about what a person hopes or expects to do in the future are equally integral to this sense of self-identity. In tragic narratives people typically responded to questions about why they found unemployment distressing by pointing to their inability to attain their hopes for the future. In contrast to the strong romance narratives, where people first told a detailed story about their past, in tragic narratives people typically began by describing a detailed life plan for their future. These imagined futures, however, were constructed as continuations of previous identities and commitments, with unemployment appearing as a disruption to the desired story of their lives.

Ricoeur (1992:177) points out that life plans are worked out as people negotiate between more generalised ideals or values and concrete practical strategies. A life plan to be a worker generally represents the influence of several, more or less abstract, ideals. In the interviews many people argued for the value of working in a generalised sense, often linked to the idea that they should be contributing something to society. People also described values associated with creativity and self-expression that shaped the specific jobs they would prefer. However, these values often conflicted with more pragmatic concerns about finances, and the pressing need to obtain any form of employment.

All the interviews contain stories about a preferred work career. This story about a preferred work career forms the ideal toward which people struggle in their attempts to find work. I use 'life plans' more generally to include work careers, anticipated relationships with family, friends, and various other imagined future activities. Work careers were typically central to people's life plans. Some of the stories about preferred work careers were described as unattainable dreams. Other people hoped, to varying degrees, that their dreams were attainable and realizable. Preferred work careers such as, for example, a fishing guide or an artist, typically draw on ideals associated with self-expression, freedom, and creativity. On the other hand, concerns about money and 'doing something', led people to more pragmatic expectations about the sort of work they might find.

It is the tension between these ideals and actual experiences that is the source of the desire to move forward in search of a more satisfying identity, and also the source of depression and despair. The preferred work career was often implied in a self-label such as 'I am a corporate manager'. However, this self-label is, in some senses, false when the person is not working as a corporate manager and may never do so again. 'This falseness is neither accidental nor a liability, as some critics imply; it is essential. The endeavour to extinguish the falseness - the subject's longing to become identical with its story - is the impetus to development' (Rosenwald 1992:286). I would add that the inability to extinguish this falseness is at the heart of the tragic experience of what it means to be unemployed - a status defined by the person not being what they want to be.

Polkinghorne (1988:106) suggests that people become depressed because they are unable to narrate a valued life plan. However, I argue that it is not a simple absence of a life plan that is problematic. Rather, it is the inability to attain an ideal life plan that causes the stress associated with tragic unemployment. Interviewees told stories about both what they hoped or wished would happen, and, on the other hand, what they expected or feared might happen if their current unemployed state continued. The tragedy lies in the inconsistency between idealised hopes and more probable expectations reflected in current actual experiences.

Rob had been retrenched from two jobs in the twelve months prior to his interview. The first of these job loss events had the form of a traumatic tragedy. He was twenty-six years old when I interviewed him and had been employed for most of his career as a labourer on construction sites. Rob describes clearly the distresses associated with the contradiction between an imagined work career and an actual status as unemployed:

Rob: I'd been unemployed for what, about two and a half years now till this scaffolding crowd came along and he put me on wages, he was putting on a few blokes ... I was over the moon even though I'd put on weight and I was unfit, I was able to cope because that adrenaline of getting a job, getting back on wages, back in the construction, I mean the situation was ideal. And one week to the day he sacked us all. Now this was the hardest thing. I was really sick in the stomach, depressed and I felt real bad and I was very annoyed.

Doug: Why do you think you felt so bad?

Rob: I think because this supreme, [pause] in that it was sudden and because I was really riding on a high as in I could feel myself being driven by some sort of excitement that I'd got back in with everything, the RDOs [rostered days off] and I'm on wages and I don't have to worry, I'd like to go in and do my work and take home a fair day's pay and at the end of the year I'll be on annual leave and take holidays and that's what I love.

Doug: So there was a sense of a future and plans and structure and that sort of thing?

Rob: Yes, that's exactly it. Because straight away my mind races at a hundred miles an hour with plans of I'll be able to get this, and I'll be able to buy this, and I'll be able to do this and I'll be able to get more materials and more tools for when, say, if it doesn't last ... That's why it became such a kick in the guts.

Rob identifies two sources of the distress he experienced as a consequence of his sacking. First, it was 'sudden'. This unprincipled way of sacking Rob clearly caused considerable anguish, and this aspect of job loss is discussed further below. Second, Rob emphasises the loss of his anticipated future as the main source of his distress. He was employed on 'wages'. This implied a permanent position with security, the development of long term relationships and a regular routine to the day, the week and the year. Further, having work would enable him to buy materials and tools to support his building hobby. These imagined futures are ruined by being sacked. These imagined futures are also developed out of, and consistent with, various past identities. Rob had been cultivating a building hobby for some time, as a constructive activity to keep him occupied whilst unemployed. His anticipated pleasure in routines also had its source in memories of earlier work experiences.

In Rob's case the experiences of working and being unemployed were brought into sharp contrast by his very short period of employment. However, it was not only people who had been recently employed who found their imagined futures destroyed by being sacked. Charles had been an executive manager with The Mining Company for 25 years. He also rationalises his decision not to take a lower paid, lower status job that was offered him because of what it would mean for his future:

Charles: So there was a job in the final analysis, but I didn't take it.

Doug: And what was the main reason that you didn't take it?

Charles: I felt that to stay would mean, [pause] I believed that career wise my career with them had finished. I mean, if they were this ambivalent towards me as a person, not knowing strongly whether they wanted me or not, you know, I felt that my prospects in that organisation were very mediocre.

Charles' decision to leave is not explained as the result of dissatisfaction with his job in the present. Rather, he is dissatisfied with his career prospects that are central to his imagined future. Further, it was the loss of this future that was the main source of his distress once he became unemployed. Middle class managers often experience considerable stress when their career advancement is impeded (Ochberg 1988:176), and

Charles' account is clearly consistent with this pattern. Charles' reported work history consisted mostly of a series of his manoeuvres to advance his career. His imagined future grew out of experiences that had been central to his past life.

Charles' account also indicates that some forms of employment may be experienced as inconsistent with a preferred work career. Charles chose to leave The Mining Company because the work that they were offering him was inconsistent with his preferred work career. That is to say, working in an occupation that is experienced as oppressive or grossly inappropriate can also threaten a person's sense of self and lead to depression and anxiety. This point is discussed in more detail later in the Chapter.

Job loss ruins a person's hopes for their imagined future as a worker. The imagined work career gives the future structure and organisation, enabling the person to map a trajectory through life, anticipating what will be required of them and providing a sense of self-sameness consistent with their past. While the specific content of a preferred work career can take various forms, everyone in this study emphasised that this imagined future would solve many of their central concerns about working and life in general. Tragic job loss represents a moment when the events of lived experience ruin the plausibility of this narrative. In summary, the implausibility of a desired future is a central source of distress for people who narrate their job loss as a tragedy.

McCall and Simmons (1967:165) point out that when a person's life plan is disrupted, 'whether by others or by himself [sic.], his whole enterprise of identity legitimation is threatened until he can work out a new, "next best" answer to the staging problems posed by his variety of desired role-performances'. The difficulty of finding a new job or some other solution to unemployment, means that unemployment is often experienced as a sustained attack on central narrative-identities that legitimate a person's relationships with family, friends, and society in general. In other words, an imagined future work career is an integrally social story. This has two aspects. First, relationships with other people often rely on the person being employed, and sometimes more specifically, employed in a particular type of job. Second, the desire to work, and the centrality of working to the self concept, are an internalised reflection of public narratives about the importance of working. These points will be discussed in turn.

A narrative of self-identity is also a story of how a person will interact with other people. Relationships with other people are often premised on being a worker. For example, Lyn described how being unemployed distanced her from her friends:

Doug: Thinking of your five most important friends, can you tell me what they do?

Lyn: Well actually nearly all, I think all of my friends are working actually ... and, like, they're all getting jobs and I just feel I really want to get a job and I feel, because they've all got jobs I just think I've got to get a job. Like, I feel like I'm left behind sort of.

Other respondents found that work had an even more powerful effect on their relationships with close friends and relatives. Vince, a recently married twenty-seven year old male described how losing his job as a supermarket storeman undermined an important foundation of his relationship with his partner Merryn:

Vince: When I lost the storeman job I actually came home and cried, I was really upset about it. It was because Merryn's parents were here for Christmas and I found out Christmas Eve, you know, 'Merry Christmas, you're sacked' ... And you know, for a while it was lookin' like yeah, we're going to be normal, in that hell called normality, for a while. And I felt I was letting down her parents and her and it wasn't my fault. I was pissed off, I was angry but I was most of all upset.

For Vince losing his job destroyed the image of self as a worker, on which his relationships with Merryn and her parents were premised. As argued in Chapter Three, a network of secure social bonds is required to sustain a positive sense of self. Losing a job frequently severs or threatens these social bonds. Shame and depression occur as a result of the consequent threat to the intersubjective supports for a person's central identities.

Further, not only does Vince feel he has failed in his responsibilities to his spouse and her parents, but he has also lost his opportunity to be 'normal'. Vince protects his self-esteem by distancing himself from the idea of 'normality' by calling it a 'hell'. However, the fact that he cannot be a 'normal' person with a job is clearly a source of distress for Vince. The idea of 'normality' suggests the importance of working as part of a much broader cultural discourse. That is to say, stories about a preferred work career are clearly derived from, and consistent with, public narratives or cultural repertoires about the value of work.

Public narratives or cultural repertoires about the importance of working are sustained through a variety of mediums including television and educational experiences. Seabrook (1982:25) describes clearly the effect of television on unemployed people's self-perceptions. It is not just that television advertises goods such as lawn mowers, cars, American Express cards and holidays that are clearly unattainable:

On the screen there is a sustained intensity of emotions, but expansive, passionate emotions, lust and greed, love and violence; not the irritation and tetchiness of a domestic interior. The televisions seemed to disturb their lives by this insistence on stormy and powerful relationships, more often than not allied to great wealth. The week I was there an American four-part serial seemed to shriek at Mike and Jean their own inadequacy. I had the impression that they felt their life was diminished, their relationship denied. *Their own experience is nowhere validated publicly.* (Seabrook 1982:15, emphasis added)

A life plan is not only a story about desired work and relationships, it is also a story about participating in other socially valued activities. Work, and particularly the money that comes from working, are very important because they enable a person to sustain a wide variety of social relationships including marriage, going out to night clubs, paying off a car loan, and taking a turn paying for the tennis court hire. These activities are important because they provide the person with a sense of worth that is publicly validated. Losing a job and being unemployed are defined by what a person does *not* have or does *not* do. Public narratives, conveyed by the expectations of friends or the television, emphasise the value of working and of being able to have the possessions and leisure activities that are associated with working.

Public narratives become internalised and part of a person's internal dialogue. The internal dialogue is a central arena where a person narrates their experience and forms a sense of self-identity. In interviews people often described their thoughts whilst explaining their decisions and interpretations of events. They described conversations with themselves rather than conversations with other people. The quotation from Lyn provided earlier is a good example. Discussing how she felt after she lost her job, she emphasises her thoughts: 'I just thought "where am I going", I just thought "what am I doing with my life?"' This socially constructed internalised dialogue is the arena in which people's interpretations and understandings of the job loss event are formed and sustained.

In summary, tragic job loss narratives are characterised by an inconsistency between the actualities of lived experience and a desired life plan. A life plan develops out of past identities and stretches into an imagined future. Life plans are developed in interaction with others, and are sustained in an internal dialogue or soliloquy. Desired work careers are typically central to these life plans. Job loss ruins at least temporarily, a person's planned work career, and therefore their life plan. Threatened social relationships, and the loss of important markers of self-identity all serve to undermine a person's narrative-identities that provide a sense of purpose and place in society. In short, the threat that unemployment poses to a person's narrative-identity is the main source of emotional distress in tragic accounts of job loss.

Tragic Job Loss: Four Variations on a Theme

Not all job losses are equally destructive of a person's life plan. The way in which a person loses their job, and whether the last job was oppressive or enjoyable influences a person's understanding of job loss and the effect it has on their life plan. Differences in these factors form the basis of four variants of the tragic job loss narrative: traumatic tragedies, moderated tragedies, ironic tragedies, and sustained tragedies. All share the same sharply felt inconsistency between being unemployed and the imagined ideal of being employed, but differ in the form of retrenchment and in the evaluation of the previous job. The remainder of this Chapter discusses these types of tragedies in detail.

The difference between traumatic and moderated job loss narratives is pictured graphically in Figure 4. The way a person is retrenched can add to, or moderate, the trauma of job loss. Very short notice, inappropriate timing, and the humiliating events associated with losing a job can all create anger and distress as a consequence of a violently disturbed life plan. On the other hand, a long notice period, counselling, monetary retrenchment packages, and outplacement services that help the person begin to find work, can all moderate the impact of the job loss allowing the person to renegotiate their life plan.

Ironic tragedies constitute a third form of tragic narratives. Ironic tragedies involve a changing perception of the last job. Leaving is chosen, desired, and celebrated. However, unemployment is experienced as surprisingly oppressive and deeply distressing. From a retrospective point of view the job that was left becomes increasingly attractive and people express regret at having left this job. The tragedy is ironic because the very act that was intended to bring freedom results in a more painful situation.

Finally, tragedies may be sustained tragedies. Sustained tragedies also involve leaving or losing an oppressive job. However, unlike ironic tragedies, there is no sense of regret or surprise in the experience of unemployment. The unpleasantness of unemployment was anticipated, but still seen as preferable to the last job. These narratives are sustained tragedies because of the stark inconsistency between an imagined ideal future work career and both the last job and the current unemployed status. Both the last job and being unemployed are tragic reminders of the person's inability to attain an ideal work career.

Figure 4   Moderated and traumatic tragic job loss narratives

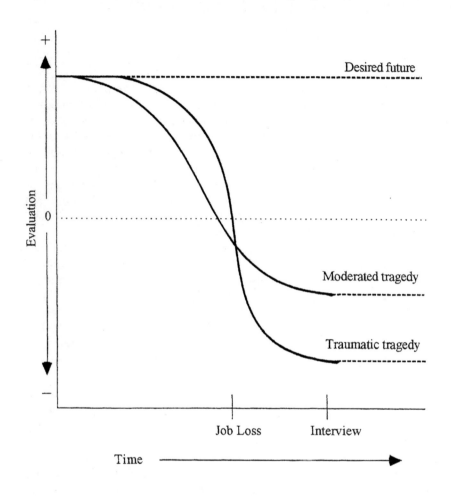

Job Loss as a Traumatic Tragedy

Scholes and Kellog (1966:236) suggest that the classical understanding of tragedy as a product of a fatal flaw or 'harmatia' is transformed in modern fiction into the destruction of the individual due to trauma. Tragic narratives typically contain an account of the trauma of being sacked. Of the twenty-four tragedies, fifteen described major injustices on the part of the management during their job loss. Six of these narratives I describe as traumatic tragedies because the trauma associated with the job loss event is central to their experience.

Traumatic tragic job loss is characterised by a sharp decline in self-evaluations immediately following the job loss (see Figure 4). As argued earlier, low self-evaluations are a consequence of the grief associated with losing a satisfying job and the desirable future it had promised. However, the vexatious management of the retrenchment magnified the distress caused by the job loss. These people were all very angry with their employers. They all had less than one day's notice and were sacked at difficult or unexpected times. Some were given notice during or just before a Christmas party, others after having been told their work would continue for much longer. The financial consequences of these sackings were also often serious, especially when some employers did not pay people what they were owed. Lyn's account of her sacking describes clearly the traumatic consequences of what she considered a tactless handling of her retrenchment by management:

Doug: When did you know that it [your job] was going to finish up?
Lyn: Well I didn't really. I came into work as usual on the Wednesday and I was just told that basically they didn't want me any more. I didn't know anything about it and I was, and then I sort of went to my desk and it was like somebody else was using my computer, and I just thought, what's going on, I was called into the office and they just basically told me that they didn't want me any more and they wanted someone with more experience ... like I couldn't really say much at the time because I was pretty upset and I was trying to control myself from not bursting into tears and I was trying not to be really angry either. And I just thought like what am I going to do now. So I sort of felt like this is not happening, I'm dreaming this, this is a nightmare.

When a job loss is not anticipated it does not give the person the opportunity to make adjustments to their activities and self-narrative that may smooth the transition. A long notice period allows a form of anticipatory socialisation in which some of the potentially threatening aspects of the transition can be neutralised and a new life plan negotiated. The unanticipated nature of these traumatic transitions makes the shock of sudden change extremely disruptive.

Similar patterns have been observed in studies of divorce and bereavement. In the case of divorcees, researchers have found that the shorter the period of preparation, the greater the difficulties for the divorcee in adjusting to the new status (Kitson et al. 1989). Kohen (1981:235) suggests that anticipation and preparation enables adjustments to divorce because they allow the person to relinquish the marital role prior to separation. Preparation time is also an important predictor of the severity of the effect of bereavement. Riley, (1983) for example, separates 'lingering' deaths from unexpected accidents. In the former case, such as deaths associated with terminal illnesses, recovery of the bereaved person appears to be facilitated by the preparation time that allows the person to begin to redefine his or her role and to assume new responsibilities prior to the death. 'In contrast, unexpected accidents and most suicides are found to produce the most severe bereavement reactions: shock, bewilderment, despair, and often physical illness. In such cases, where widows must make sense of a world that has suddenly lost its meaning, recovery tends to be a long process and is frequently accompanied by overwhelming sorrow and loss of the sense of personal control' (Riley 1983:205).

The absence of notice or anticipation was also important when the job loss caused financial distress. Two of the six people who narrated their job loss as a traumatic tragedy had adapted to living on unemployment benefits and did not feel stressed as a result of their job loss. However, the other four people described themselves as in financial difficulties almost immediately after their job loss. The combination of no notice and not being paid what he was due resulted in one respondent being evicted from his flat because he could not afford to pay his rent. A longer notice period may have given this person time to manage his finances more effectively. Alternatively, a more generous retrenchment payment may also have reduced the trauma of the loss. Thus, slender financial resources combined with no notice resulted in the job loss being severely disruptive.

People in this group all described the tasks of their last job as highly satisfying. Work was greatly valued and a clear source of high self esteem. They also typically describe the job loss as leaving them socially isolated. For these people work was a very important source of friendships and social interaction. In other words, work was valued both as a worthwhile activity in itself, and as a source of friendship and social interaction. This understanding of their last job reinforced an image of working as pleasurable that stood in stark contrast to their experience of unemployment. Feelings of depression and distress were reinforced by the fracturing of social relationships both inside and outside the workplace. Vince's account of the effects of his Christmas sacking on relationships with his family as described earlier in the Chapter is a clear example of the stress sudden retrenchment places on relationships, and the consequent effects on a person's sense of self-worth.

The way in which these people were retrenched by management implied they were incompetent, worthless, and not worth treating with respect. In the early parts of Vince's interview he describes a number of times how the management 'treat[s] everyone like shit', particularly with reference to the way he was sacked. Later in the interview it becomes clear that Vince has internalised this image of himself as a worthless 'shit-kicker'. However, Vince also tries to exploit a common neutralising strategy: condemning the condemners (Sykes and Matza 1957:668). The managers were condemned as immoral and unprincipled. The job loss could therefore be described as a consequence of the manager's immoral behaviour rather than any deficiency on the part of the narrator. Vince's experience is discussed in more detail in the next Chapter. Other people struggled in similar ways with the negative implications of the way they were retrenched.

In summary, a high level of job satisfaction, combined with retrenchment without notice and financial distress all reinforce the severity of the trauma of job loss. These properties of the passage demolish the routines and social and financial foundations that sustained the plausibility of the person's desired life plan. They also reinforce narratives that suggest the person is worthless. Unemployment is a liminal devalued status that offers few, if any, rewards. Working is central to a person's narrative-identity and for these people the only conceivable source of a restored sense of self-esteem is to find another job.

Job Loss as a Moderated Tragedy

Moderated job loss provides a less traumatic entry into unemployment (Figure 4). Nine people narrated their job loss in the form of a moderated tragedy. This group also described the tasks of their last job as satisfying and enjoyable. However, in contrast to the very short notice of traumatic tragedies, people who narrated their job loss as a moderated tragedy all had at least one month's notice or were employed on a short term contract. In other words, anticipation is central to the degree of trauma associated with a job loss. A long notice period reduces significantly the trauma of job loss.

Other factors also moderated the trauma of the job loss. The people in this category were typically not financially stressed, although if they remained unemployed they expected to soon be stressed. Strong friendships outside the work environment were often supportive, although some people still described themselves as socially isolated as a consequence of the job loss. Four people still respected their managers, but five were angry at how their retrenchment had been managed. While other factors helped to moderate the trauma of job loss, the length of notice was central to the strategies used to moderate the effects of the job loss.

One of the main consequences of a long notice period was that it provided a person time to reinterpret their future. Mary was a nurse who was retrenched when a large hospital closed. The three month notice period was used by the staff to talk about finishing at almost every opportunity:

Mary: So a lot of the girls would be, someone would come in really upset and they would have looked at more bills that were due and they would say how are we going to cope. We used to sort of talk all the time about it. Which was good. So I definitely think it's the only way things heal and get aired.

Talking about the impact of their impending retrenchment appears to have allowed Mary, and her co-workers, the opportunity to re-imagine their futures. To begin to anticipate some of the problems they would encounter, including how to pay bills, and to try to work out some coping strategies for dealing with these problems. Mary explicitly identifies this as a social process.

Not only did Mary and her co-workers talk amongst themselves, they also had access to the services of a counsellor to help them come to terms with their retrenchment. From her discussions with this counsellor, Mary had come to understand her experience as a grief process. This understanding was based on an interpretation of Kubler Ross' (1969) discussion of aspects (Mary did not see them as consecutive stages) of grief to make sense of her feelings of loss, anger, denial and depression. She felt that she was now coming to a stage of acceptance and that she was ready to work at getting another job:

Doug: How do you feel about not being with work?
Mary: I miss it, I miss the people. I do, I miss it. But it's happened, I can't change that and now I've got to go about getting out into the work force and seeing what's out there for me now.

This quotation from Mary is indicative of the higher levels of confidence and hope characteristic of moderated tragedies, as indicated in Figure 4. While moderated tragedies did result in a more optimistic and positive outlook, the research was not designed to provide an assessment of whether this enabled people to obtain another job more easily than those who experienced traumatic tragedies. This proposition has initial plausibility because higher self-esteem is conducive both to more vigorous job search activities and better presentation in interviews, both of which would improve the chances of obtaining work (Markus and Nurius 1986:962). This point was also made by one of the interviewees. While people in this moderated job loss category found that job loss undermined some of their friendships, particularly as a consequence of their severely limited financial situation, the long notice period allowed people to negotiate short term coping strategies that helped them avoid the more unpleasant sudden disruptions to relationships characteristic of traumatic narratives. Earlier I argued that identities are not created in isolation, but are intersubjective constructions. The renegotiation of plans and relationships provided ongoing social support for a stronger sense of self-continuity than was possible in traumatic tragedies.

However, a moderated easing into unemployment does not prevent people from experiencing the full range of depression and anxiety associated with remaining unemployed. While people who narrated their experience of unemployment as a moderated tragedy began their unemployment on a more positive note, some who had been unemployed for longer periods recounted episodes of significant depression. These experiences are discussed fully in the next Chapter.

In summary, a long notice period, combined with supportive social relationships and the absence of severe financial distress (although this often threatened to soon occur) moderated the consequences of job loss. These properties of the passage enabled people to renegotiate relationships and life plans that in turn sustained a stronger sense of self-worth that was not present in the more harrowing traumatic job loss narratives. However, unemployment was still undesirable and disruptive. The renegotiated plans were short term strategies that protected the person from the worst effects of unemployment. The search for employment was also a search for the basis of a longer term life plan that would sustain a more positive self-image.

Job Loss as an Ironic Tragedy

White (1973:9) suggests that in tragedies there are no festive occasions 'except false or illusory ones'. This is precisely the experience in ironic tragic narratives. The celebration of escaping an oppressive job turns out to be illusory. Three of the interviewees' narratives are ironic tragedies. The job loss is ironic in the sense that typically the person chose to leave their last job hoping to improve their situation. However, the very act that was intended to bring release actually resulted in a considerably worse situation, that of being unemployed for a significant period of time. As is illustrated in Figure 5, this job loss narrative follows the same tragic pattern of decline after the job loss and describes an unrealised preferred work career against which the current unemployed status is compared.

Figure 5   Job loss as an ironic tragedy

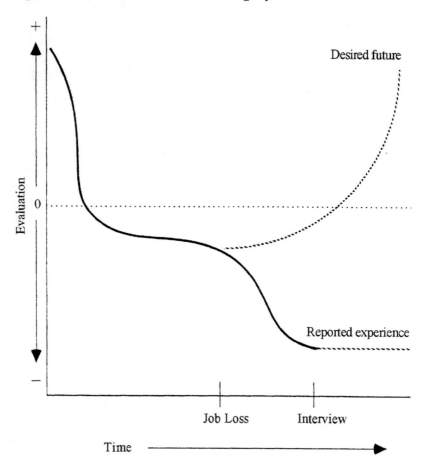

In ironic tragic job loss narratives people characterized the tasks and management of their last job in various, and often apparently contradictory ways. During the explanation of why the person chose to leave, various aspects of the job task and attitudes of management were frequently described as oppressive and given as reasons for leaving. However, other comments about what their work had involved typically depicted their job as rewarding and satisfying, assessments that resurfaced in discussions of how they felt about their last job after a period of unemployment. In other words, the evaluation of their last job appeared to have changed significantly over their time of unemployment.

Central to the experience of ironic tragedies is the discrepancy between an anticipated experience of unemployment, particularly with reference to chances in the job market, and the actual experience of unemployment. These people left their job because they wanted to escape an oppressive work environment, not because they had a concrete, well thought through plan about how they would find another job. Specific reasons for leaving included insufficient remuneration, stressful workplaces, and the fear of being sacked without a redundancy package. While the financial incentive of a redundancy package was something that enticed two of these people to leave, a redundancy package does not provide a plan for obtaining another job, nor does it typically provide long-term financial security.

Agnes was fifty-three years old when I interviewed her. She last worked as a secretary to a sectional manager of a large government owned corporation. She mostly enjoyed her last job. However, a push to 'downsize' resulted in her work environment becoming very stressful. Stress was generated both by the uncertainty of who she would be working with and what she would be doing, and by the uncertainty of whether there would be a job for her at all. She left when she decided to accept an offer of a redundancy package:

Doug: You took a package because?
Agnes: Because I thought, as we all thought, that next time around they'd just say go and there wouldn't be a package ... And I really got sick of it, I really did. But they sent me an offer of a package through the post, they didn't even have the courtesy to tell the manager, they just do things so badly. So when I came home we sat down and thought seriously about it and we thought 'well shall we take the money and run and grab this little bit of money or should I stay with all this stress, not knowing from one day to the next when we'll be closed down. So I thought I'd take it. Plus the fact that I don't know what they're going to do with our superannuation, so at least I got my contributions back ... So I had a nice, sort of little bit of money there as well which I thought would never be spent. So that was the other reason that I took it. But with regrets.

Implied in Agnes' story is a stronger version of her decision to leave that celebrated her escape from an oppressive work environment. This interpretation is supported elsewhere in the interview where she describes how she actively sought a redundancy package. However, Agnes does not develop this interpretation in detail because it would be inconsistent with the interpretation she now gives to those events. Her understanding of her choice to leave is now coloured by the experience of unemployment. The phrasing in the sentence 'nice, sort of little bit of money ... which I thought would never be spent' suggests the complexity of her understanding of her decision to leave, where past explanations are overlaid with more recent understandings. It seems clear, however, that it was only after leaving that she discovered how difficult it would be to find a job.

The choice to leave was justified both as a consequence of the desire to escape an oppressive or devalued work environment and in terms of an expectation of being able to find a better and more attractive job. However, as Agnes began to struggle with being unemployed and the jobs that were available to her, the criteria for an acceptable job began to change to the extent that the job that she had left became an attractive position. The main problem for Agnes was that her financial resources were diminishing:

Doug: Why was losing your job stressful?

Agnes: Probably because of, I don't know if I'll get another job. If I could have left [my last job] and walked into another job I would have then had this little nest egg ... I don't want my package money to go on rent, I want to keep it for us. So that I think is the main problem, I've got this terrible fear that I won't get a job, and I've also got this fear of a new environment, getting used to new bosses.

The change in tense is important in the above quote. The question is past tense, the response is present tense. Agnes suggests in another place that at the time she left her job she was pleased. However, after having left her job she became increasingly unsettled about her decision. The reasons for her stress are all in the present tense and emphasise her ongoing experience of unemployment. All the tragic ironic narratives describe unemployment as highly distressing as a result of financial troubles, or social isolation.

'Regrets' is a recurring theme in Agnes's interview, particularly when she explains why she accepted her package and how she felt after leaving. 'Regret' indicates the ironic nature of these tragic accounts. Agnes, and the other two people in this category, chose to leave their last job. Once they became unemployed they began to see that their last job, whilst unpleasant, had been significantly more satisfying than being unemployed. A few weeks after leaving her job Agnes developed agoraphobic symptoms and was referred to a therapist by her local doctor. At the time I interviewed her she described herself as 'getting very much better'. She explained the causes of her agoraphobia in the following way: 'I think it was mainly regret that I left, not so much a wealthy job but a safe job. But of course it isn't safe, it's just like being in private enterprise, you don't know when the axe is going to fall. But I think I have a lot of regrets'.

Agnes struggled for a sense of self-sameness and identity in her narrative. The decision to leave her last job is a strongly discordant note in her attempt to make sense of her current situation. The problem lies precisely in the ongoing and in-process nature of self-narratives. When Agnes finds another job she may, if the job is a good one, decide that leaving was an excellent decision, reinterpret her feelings during unemployment as an insignificant hiatus and restore some of her presently devalued reasons for leaving her last job. However, the problem with Agnes' current experience is not only that her decision to leave is discordant, but that a future as an unemployed person is strongly discordant with her desires and hopes.

In summary, the choice to leave an oppressive job followed by a highly distressing experience of unemployment results in two contradictory narratives of job loss. At the time, the choice to leave the previous job was probably justified by a narrative that romanticised expectations about the person's future job prospects. However, once unemployed these expectations were proven to be illusory and the consequences of the choice to leave become increasingly distressing as a result of being unable to find employment, financial troubles, and social isolation. These properties of the passage sustain the tragic form of the narrative. Further, these properties only begin to influence the person after they have left their job. The timing of these experiences means that a narrative that may have begun as a romance turns into a cruelly ironic tragedy.

Job Loss as a Sustained Tragedy

Eight of the narratives have a form that I describe as sustained tragedies. These narratives do not initially appear to be tragedies because they do not contain the sharp decline in self-evaluations characteristic of the tragic form. As indicated in Figure 6, these stories begin from a low point and job loss typically results in a marginal improvement in self-evaluations. However, while the story does not contain a sharp decline in self-evaluations, I argue that these are still tragic narratives. At the heart of a tragic narrative is the inconsistency between a preferred work career and the person's actual experience. In sustained tragedies both unemployment and the person's last job were strongly inconsistent with this preferred work career. All the interviewees in this category narrated a clear story about what a good job should be like, that was also part of a story about an imagined and strongly desired future work career. In some cases there was also a time in the past when the person had worked in what they saw as a 'good' job. It was the comparison between this preferred work career and their actual experiences that was the source of their depression and despair. The person's last job, their unemployment and feared future of ongoing unemployment, were paltry and painful in comparison to this imagined work career.

Figure 6   Job loss as a sustained tragedy

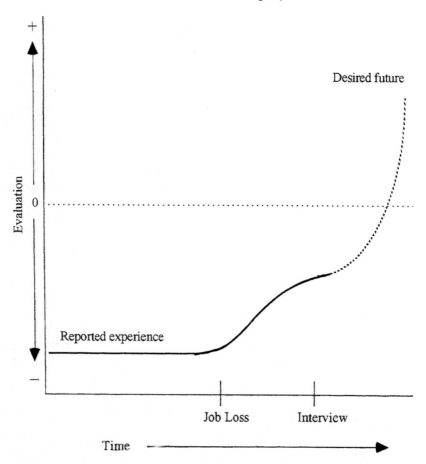

Sustained tragedies begin with a description of the markedly oppressive nature of the last job. From this perspective, while unemployment was unpleasant, leaving or losing their last job was still a positive move. Even unemployment was seen as preferable to the conditions of their last job. People in this category rarely had a positive word to say about their last job or their employers. The work task, for example, was depicted as boring, dangerous, or extremely burdensome. The managers were typically portrayed as inconsiderate, abusive, and incompetent.

Strong dissatisfaction with the last job was also consistent with the person's attitudes toward former work associates who typically were not close friends and often characterized as hostile. Five of the eight interviewees did not feel socially isolated as a result of their job loss. Their main friends were typically outside the work environment. Few close or regular friendships had been derived from their previous workplace, and most had worked at maintaining their distance from work colleagues. Of the three who did feel socially isolated, this isolation was a product of being unable to pay for their usual social outings rather than because they had lost close social friendships from their previous workplace. In short, the negative evaluation of the last job was consistent across social relationships, the work task, and attitudes toward management.

Allan was thirty-one years old when interviewed and had been working for the previous two years as a 'houseman' at a large hotel. His job mainly involved setting up for functions and conferences and cleaning up afterwards. Allan described the management as oppressive, abusive, and inconsiderate. He recounted being required to work very long shifts in busy times and then not receiving enough work to survive financially in quiet periods. Whilst working at the hotel Allan began to experience severe headaches, chest pains, and generally felt very stressed and anxious. Allan's job at the hotel finally ended after management changed their mind about Allan taking a week of holidays over Christmas. He refused to work, and after that his job ended. After a few weeks his headaches and chest pains subsequently disappeared.

Doug: So you left, and it sounds as if that's been a reasonably positive experience?
Allan: Oh well I still get uptight and anxious because I'm not working, but I realise that if I had stayed at The Hotel my health would have gone down the gurgler even faster. I mean, I couldn't imagine anyone wanting to be unemployed. Not by choice. I sort of realise that if I, certainly I had the choice to stay there or quit, my health was more important and my sanity was more important. I found I was getting very aggressive in the last couple of months while I was working, which is, I mean, I'm not an aggressive person except at the footy. Now, it was positive in the sense that I got away from that. The negative side is obviously I've got to find

>another job and I have to find a job at a place where I can stay ... Where I
>can stay for the next how many years I am working.

This quotation captures the two major features of sustained tragedies.
First, work was very unpleasant, and while unemployment is also
unpleasant, the last job was even worse. Allan recounted how the damaging
effect the job was having on his health had led his flat mate to threaten
to 'break his legs' if he continued to work there. When asked what his
flat mate thought of him being unemployed, Allan said: 'Oh he feels it's
better than to be working at The Hotel'. From this perspective there
was no room for a sense of regret at having left or lost his previous job.
All who were asked whether they would be prepared to consider working
again in their previous job responded with a clear 'no'. The main source
of anger with the conditions of their last job varied. Some people felt
they were grossly underpaid, others were required to perform dangerous
tasks or found the management so abusive and incompetent that they
'could not bear it'. However, as noted above, dissatisfaction was typically
broadly based and the person's last job possessed few, if any, redeeming
features.

Second, these narratives all contain a clear account of a preferred
work career that stands in stark contrast to both unemployment and the
previous job. Allan, for example, wanted to find a permanent and secure
job so that he could buy a house and settle down: 'You've got to have
security and you've got to prove yourself and I'll do whatever it takes,
I'll go back and do courses, I'll do whatever I have to so long as I can
have a secure job, and some good money, and I've got a future'. As
argued earlier, it is the failure to achieve this ideal that makes a narrative
tragic. In Allan's case he had begun to wonder whether, at thirty-one, he
would ever be able to establish himself because of repeated messages
from employers that he was 'too old'.

While some people had worked in what they described as a 'good job'
at some stage in the past, the image of the preferred work career clearly
had its most significant source in cultural repertoires that defined what a
'good' life plan should be like. Three men in their mid thirties, for
example, talked about the link between having a job and being able to
sustain a relationship with a view to marriage. One man specifically
attributed his break-up with his last girlfriend to the unsatisfactory nature
of his last job and his unemployment. All three men linked hopes about
marriage and having a family to finding secure employment. This image
of a 'good life' as including marriage and children had clear social sources.
Two men, for example, reported conversations with parents about the
importance of marriage. In other words, the content of a preferred

work career and the broader life plan were influenced by cultural repertoires that define a 'good life'. The gendered nature of the meaning of working is discussed in more detail in Chapter Eight.

All of the interviewees whose narratives are sustained tragedies anticipated the ending of their last job, typically because they had wanted it to finish for some time. Although some of these people had only very short periods of official notice, it was clear that the end of the job was not a surprise. Further, most of the people had some degree of influence over the termination of their employment. As the above quote from Allan indicates, it is often unclear whether the person chose to leave or was sacked, or perhaps provoked the management into sacking them. The lack of clarity about the cause of the job loss in some narratives may reflect an attempt to hide the cause of the job loss in order to preserve 'face' (Goffman 1967). However, it may also simply reflect the complexity of the events.

Sustained tragedies are doubly tragic. Both the last job and unemployment are harrowing because the person fails to attain their preferred work career. The image of a 'good job' contained in the story about a preferred work career is the basis of their justification for leaving, or being pleased to lose, their previous job. This celebrated ending of their last job sits uneasily with the consequences of being without work. Unemployment is also distressing because only a 'good job' provides the financial and social rewards that can sustain a longer term life plan. The desired life plan is a social creation, reflecting the influence of close friends, and more general cultural repertoires. Not fulfilling this life plan also has social implications, resulting in restricted interactions and the breakdown of some important relationships. While leaving their last job marginally improved most people's social life, being unemployed still threatened to disrupt any new social networks that a person attempted to enter.

In summary, the inability to find a 'good job' is the main source of the person's despair and devalued sense of self. On the other hand, a life plan and the associated preferred work career can also be a source of hope and inspiration in a dark time. The next Chapter examines in detail the experience of unemployment and the movement between hope, despair, and sullen resignation.

Doug: So the financial consequences of being unemployed are pretty difficult.
Allan: Oh yeah. Very hard. Your pay pack stops. You get money from Social Security but ... it's still hard. And in a way it's degrading, thinking that you're not working, and you see everybody else working and you think,

gee I could do that. But I guess I've just got to get out and prove myself and hope that somebody will give me the chance to prove myself.

Conclusion

Depression, anxiety, and low self-esteem experienced after a job loss can be understood as a consequence of the tragic form of the narrative of the job loss. In these narratives unemployment is described as threatening central social relationships and a person's long term life plan. Properties of the passage, such as the length of notice and the level of satisfaction with the previous job, influence the form of threat to social relationships and a person's life plan. These in turn influence the specific form of the tragic narrative that may be traumatic, moderated, ironic, or sustained. Central to tragic job loss narratives is a life plan and an associated preferred work career derived from cultural repertoires and supported by interaction with close friends. The inconsistency between an imagined life plan and the current realities of unemployment and the threatened experience of ongoing unemployment is the main source of a person's distress.

6 Tragic Unemployment

Introduction

The previous Chapter focused on the trauma of losing a job while this Chapter focuses on the ordeal of being unemployed. The experience of unemployment associated with tragic job loss narratives is a liminal, or in-between, state of transition. After the trauma of losing a job, the passage of time results in the increasing importance of the pressure of being without work as the source of distress. I use the term 'tragic unemployment' to refer to this experience. People described this time as a period of emptiness and 'nothingness' when the lack of structure and the constant rejection of job applications were difficult to endure. Tragic unemployment is distressing because of the experience of being without a job whilst at the same time wanting one desperately, and with no certainty about when, or if, a job will be found. Tragic unemployment disrupts central narrative-identities and while the person remains unemployed they remain without the activity that would legitimate their claimed identity as a worker.

It is important to distinguish the experience of unemployment described in romantic narratives from the experience of unemployment described in tragic narratives. Romantic job loss narratives describe an experience of transition. However, the transitional time is not frustrating because people have a clear plan of action, and are confident they will obtain employment in the future. On the other hand, after a tragic job loss, people described themselves as not only looking for work, but looking for a plausible narrative that might provide them with some sense of hope and purpose. Tragic unemployment is painful, and depressing, because people are *not* able to find a story that gives them confidence they will find a job soon.

Three main types of response to tragic unemployment are described in the next section of this Chapter. The Chapter then outlines the general structure of the experience of tragic unemployment. The liminal nature of tragic unemployment is clearest in unemployed people's sense of having no worthwhile place in society. Next, I discuss the active search for employment as an attempt to escape this liminality. Some accounts also described more positive periods where people engaged in leisure activities designed to give structure to their day and a sense of self-worth separate from the search for employment. Following this, I examine in detail acute experiences of depression and their relationship

93

to the narrative structure of identity. Periods of self-deprecation and depression are typically associated with an attitude of resignation to the impossibility of finding a 'good job'. Finally, I explore the potential for narrating experiences of unemployment in different ways.

Tragic Unemployment: Variations in People's Experiences

Some people described cycles of positive and negative responses to unemployment. Rob, for example, described a cycle of active job search followed by resignation. He rationalises his resignation as a self-protective mechanism. The constant rejections 'build up' until he avoids looking for work because he does not want to be rejected again. Rob also has a number of hobbies that enable him to keep active and maintain a positive attitude:

Rob: I look for a job pretty hard for a couple of months, then I sort of slack a bit ... you get sick of the knockbacks all the time.
Doug: Why is it that the rejections are so hard?
Rob: I think rejection isn't so bad in normal life situations when things are pretty comfortable. But when you're unemployed and you're looking for a job ... every time you're getting told no. I mean, it's water off a duck's back because you're sort of half expecting it, you know the situation, there's not much work around. But after a while you get sick of people saying no. That's why I can do it pretty hard for a couple of months and then it builds up and it's not consciously building up but you just, you know, I'm sick of this. You're just, some days you don't bother going out there looking for work. And it ends up a couple of months when you only make a couple of phone calls. But it is a build up of rejection.

In contrast to unemployed people who described cycles of responses to unemployment, a second group were consistently more positive, and a third group were consistently more negative in their accounts of unemployment. While experiences of resignation and depression were typically associated with longer periods of unemployment, some people described this type of experience occurring immediately after their job loss. Similarly, while people who narrated a moderated tragic job loss often began their unemployment on a more positive note than those who experienced a traumatic tragic job loss, they still experienced periods of severe depression.

There are clear indicators in some interviews that the person would previously have narrated their experience in a quite different way because of significantly different conditions at that time. This is consistent with the conceptualisation of narrative-identity as formed and reformed in response to the events of lived experience. In other words, while some unemployed people explained their experience using a tragic narrative, it is possible that when they first lost their job their narrative may have had the form of a romance. Further, while some people described themselves as highly distressed and depressed, and others are more positive, these interpretations of unemployment have probably changed over time. Several people, including Rob, were consciously aware of these changes. While others did not describe their story as having changed form, it is difficult to know whether this is a consequence of a desire to avoid dissonance or a reflection of the consistency of their narrative over time. Longitudinal research is required to describe fully these temporal aspects of the changing form of people's narratives of unemployment.

This Chapter focuses predominantly on the stories of Vince and Charles whose job losses were traumatic and moderated tragedies respectively. Both were briefly mentioned in the previous Chapter. Vince was twenty-seven years old when I interviewed him and had been unemployed for twelve months. His last job was as a storeman for a large supermarket chain, and he had previously worked as a cab driver. Charles was forty-seven years old when I interviewed him and had been unemployed for six months. His last job was as a corporate manager of a large international mining company. Charles had enough money to live comfortably for the rest of his life. Vince had substantial debts with few assets. While Vince was sacked with no notice and no compensation, Charles had ample notice and a large redundancy payment. Despite these differences, both narratives share the same form of a tragedy.

Tragic Unemployment: The Distress of Being Without Employment

At the heart of most people's distress during unemployment was a sense that they were not needed by society. While some felt they had let down specific people, the sense of being not needed was more generalised. People felt a responsibility to contribute to society through working. Being unemployed, and unsuccessful job applications, suggested that their contribution was not valued by society. This is consistent with the argument developed in Chapter Three that an important contributor to the maintenance of positive self-esteem is the faithful fulfilment of commitments to others. This point is perhaps most clear in Charles' account. While Charles had an excellent resume, influential referees and financial security, he still felt that he had no place of value in society:

Doug: And so how did you feel about being unemployed?
Charles: Well, (pause).
Doug: And how did your feelings change?
Charles: The feeling um, (pause) very quickly I went into a period of feeling sort of worthless. Even though I knew dutifully I had very good credentials, excellent career record, excellent resume, excellent references. Look I had everything possibly going for me, plus the security. I still felt somehow as though I didn't have much to offer and I felt worthless for a period there. And I felt, you know, you would see people going off to work that had very mediocre jobs, and you felt, in many ways, they were more valuable to society than I was, no matter how low their jobs were. Because they had an existence. And ah, (pause) it was coming from being structured, over, right from school age to leading this life of tremendous structure and pressure to suddenly having no structure. Apart from what ... [the outplacement services] offered me. And I hate to know how I would have coped without them.

While Charles mentions the absence of structure as a source of his distress, he first mentions a sense of worthlessness derived from not working. For Charles, and for many other respondents, being unemployed was understood to imply that they were not valued by society. Charles felt he needed to work in order to fulfil an obligation to contribute to society. His sense of worthlessness whilst unemployed was partially a consequence of a feeling that he was not fulfilling this obligation to society.

The pauses in the dialogue and Charles' body language during the interview both attest to the embarrassment Charles described feeling whilst unemployed. There are three long pauses of more than two seconds in the above passage. In the rest of the interview such pauses are much less common. When Charles was telling me about his general work history he sat openly, leaning forward on the desk with arms apart and gesticulating. There were two points in the interview when he sat back and crossed his arms. First, when I asked him about his marriage break-up Charles indicated that this was a particularly painful experience. The second time Charles sat back and crossed his arms was during the above exchange when I asked about how he felt whilst unemployed. Unemployment was clearly a very difficult experience for Charles. Later in the interview we were talking about why he had not taken a holiday, but rushed into trying to find another job:

Doug: You say money was important, but was there something more to it than that?

Charles: It's feeling needed ... If you've worked, like the sorts of jobs I have, and coming from my disposition, all of a sudden, when you feel you are not wanted and you can't cope with that and you've got to get yourself back into something. Even if it's a job that pays nothing. You just are wanting someone to say, 'Here Charles, here's a job, we need you' ... It's that period of nothingness that is, (pause) the psychology going on in that period is very hard to cope with.

Describing being unemployed as a 'period of nothingness' is another way of describing the liminality of unemployment. To be employed is to have a status and, therefore, to be valued. Unlike the liminal stages of rites of passage that involved a clearly defined waiting period with a certain ending, the uncertainty of unemployment is extremely threatening. There is no certain exit from unemployment, and finding another job is something the person must do for themselves, society will not do it for them. The rejection of job applications reinforces a sense of not being wanted.

In his previous job Charles often worked 60 or 70 hours a week, leaving little time for other activities and his most important friends were almost entirely associated with work. In other words, the structure of Charles' life reflected the centrality of working to his narrative-identity. Autobiographical narratives of managerial males typically make their career the focus of their lives (Gergen 1992:134), and Charles is no exception to this pattern. The 'tremendous structure' that Charles identifies in his previous employment can be seen as referring not only to his work providing a time structure to the day, but to the way in which working had provided the structures of Charles' self-narrative. Being without work left Charles without the routines, long-term plans, and challenges around which he had structured his foundational self-narrative. A narrative-identity as a worker, and more specifically as a manager was the only conceivable basis on which Charles could construct a feeling of self-worth and a more general sense of his value to society.

While other respondents were not as totally committed to their work as Charles, they spoke of similar experiences. Alternative roles such as being a parent or recreational activities may initially provide some support and a sense of self-worth whilst unemployed. However, they are not a substitute for employment. In particular the financial troubles of unemployment caused these other roles to place mounting pressure on most unemployed people.

Allan, whose experience was discussed in the previous Chapter, pointed to the centrality of the relationship between working and the way a person imagined their future:

Allan: And you don't look forward to going up to Bali or going up to Queensland, because you haven't got the money so you can't really plan for holidays. There's no incentive. Like, if you've got a job and you're working hard and you say 'oh well, rostered day off next week so I've only got to get through this week and I've only got Monday, Tuesday, Wednesday, only three days, great'. So there's little encouragements to keep you going. When you're not working you don't get those little encouragements ... it's just, you've got to keep the momentum up all the time, week in, week out, keep up your own momentum.

The structure that work provides to a person's day, week, and year support a narrative interpretation of the future that provides a sense of purpose and a motivational incentive. Allan describes this narrative as an internal dialogue, a soliloquy. While being unemployed does not prevent a person from maintaining a sense of purpose, the soliloquy must be kept up by the person themselves without the 'momentum' provided by the regular activities of working. When a person is able to narrate a future that has a clear structure this provides a sense of coherence to his or her narrative-identity. It is the disruption of this coherent narrative-identity that makes the experience of unemployment so difficult.

Unemployment disrupts close friendships when regular meetings at work or expensive outings are forfeited. This also reinforced the feeling of not being wanted. Most respondents mentioned work friends who were unable to cope with their unemployment. Some friends actively avoided the unemployed person. Others ignored the financial constraints that being unemployed imposed on the person. Charles described three types of friends: those who were actively supportive, those who let him down, and the 'fence sitters'.

Doug: Again thinking of your more important friends. How did they respond to you leaving The Mining Company?
Charles: It's very interesting that you ask that question, because people, I found, fall into three camps. There's those who flock to your assistance ... One particular person who was actually an ex-Company person, he'd left some years earlier, above everybody else, took me under his wing and would be calling me nearly every day to see what he could do to help. But there were other people who were, I must say I was surprised, if not shocked by the lack of interest. I, in fact I don't think, somehow, they could cope. I

felt very let down. But I tried not to be too judgemental. I couldn't possibly believe over all those seven or eight years they had pretended to be allies and weren't. Maybe they did. Maybe one or two did. Maybe one or two were using my position to, as they could to better their own, to better their selves. But I'd like to think that they had some problem in coping.

Some people had been supportive of Charles through his job loss and unemployment. Supportive friends enabled people to respond more constructively to their unemployment. On the other hand, Charles suggested that the broken friendships undermined his sense of identity. People who had appeared to be 'allies' were understood to have been superficial, perhaps cynically using his friendship for personal gain. The responses of these people to Charles' unemployment undermined the unity between Charles' narrated identity and the social relationships that supported this narrative.

Severed social bonds (Scheff 1991:15) reinforce the shameful nature of the person's current status as unemployed. Most respondents described friends who had avoided them. Some respondents also recounted that after their job loss previous work colleagues had described them as lazy or worthless. Although the condemnatory attitudes of previously close friends and associates are clearly hurtful, perhaps more important are the imagined responses of other people. For example, a number of respondents reported feeling embarrassed walking around during the day. This embarrassment was typically not because of anything people actually said to them, but because of what they imagined people were thinking.

Joyce narrated her job loss as a weak romance, and her experience was described in Chapter Four. However, she was concerned that now that her holiday was over if she did not find work soon she would become depressed and distressed. In other words, her romantic narrative was fragile and threatened to become a tragedy. She described succinctly how the structure of the working day provides social interaction and helps sustain supportive friendships:

Doug: Is it the structure that's important, is it the friendships?
Joyce: It's the stimulation, but the structure means I get up and get going. And the thing that I respond to is people. It's almost as if I need to face up to someone. But it's when nobody needs me, and I think this is part of who I am in that I've given to the children, I see myself as a mother giving to the family. I've got my stimulation, enjoyment out of doing things for other people, cooking meals for other people so that's probably the very crux of it, that the structure provides the people I suppose, doesn't it?

Joyce makes the point that a structured day provides regular interaction with people that sustains a sense of a worthwhile life. Joyce contrasts her present unemployment with earlier periods of parenthood which sustained a positive sense of self-identity through the fulfilment of her family commitments. Working, she suggests, provides a similar sense of 'stimulation' through engagement with others. A narrative-identity of positive self-worth is sustained in and through regular structured relationships with others.

The activity of working is rewarding in a variety of ways. It provides social contacts, much needed money, regular, enforced exercise and a structure to the day. Working provides challenges and a sense of contributing to society. The distressing nature of unemployment is in part a consequence of the loss of these valued aspects of working. These points are similar to those made by Jahoda in her functionalist analysis of unemployment (see Chapter Two).

Jahoda argues that unemployment causes distress and lowered mental health because of the misfit between social experiences and human needs: 'people need some structure to the waking day, need an enlarged horizon beyond their primary group, need to be involved in collective effort, need to know where they stand in society and need to be active' (Jahoda 1986:26). The negative psychological effects of unemployment are therefore explained as a consequence of the individual's exclusion from an institution that meets basic psychological needs. Jahoda suggests that the functions she identifies have some genetic foundation, although she declines to pronounce with any certainty on this issue (Jahoda 1981:184).

In contrast to Jahoda's approach, and Warr's (1987) elaboration of her model, I argue that the reason these 'functions' of working are important is because of their role in sustaining a particular narrative interpretation of employment and self-identity. Jahoda and Warr explicitly exclude any consideration of the interpretative process. I argue that the relationship between the events of lived experience and their interpretation in narrative is central to the explanation of the self-evaluative consequences of unemployment. The need to be active, to have a structure to the working day, to have enlarged horizons and to be involved in collective efforts are not biologically determined needs. Rather, they are essential supports to a narrative-identity of self-worth that locates the person in society. Being unemployed threatens or removes these supports and typically results in a narrative that devalues the person.

Tragic Unemployment: Searching for Employment

In response to the stress of unemployment people typically engage in an active search for a new job. The attempt to find work involves a struggle to escape from the uncertainty and liminality of the unemployed status. I argued in the previous Chapter that it is the tension between the ideal of a 'good job' and actual experiences of unemployment that is the source of the desire to search for a new job. As Rosenwald (1992:286) puts it: 'The endeavour to extinguish the falseness - the subject's longing to become identical with its story - is the impetus to development'. The search for a job is an unemployed person's struggle to become identical with their imagined and desired life plan.

Most people's search for work began with direct attempts to find work such as applying for advertised jobs, door knocking, ringing up employers listed in the phone book, and checking with the Commonwealth Employment Service. Some of the interviewees described periods of unemployment when they 'kept active', worked hard at searching for a job, and generally felt positive about their job prospects. They typically talked about their future with some confidence that they would soon obtain a job. Whether this confidence was justified is hard to determine because people's actual job opportunities appeared to vary considerably. People who had experienced a moderated tragedy were more likely to recount such an initial positive approach to their search for a job, particularly if they had been unemployed for only a short time.

As the period of unemployment lengthened and direct methods of searching for employment proved unsuccessful some people began to explore longer term strategies to improve their chances of success in the labour market. This typically involved seeking some sort of training. Lyn, whose experience was described in the previous Chapter, lived in an area of particularly high unemployment and soon decided she needed to improve her skills:

Doug: So, what's your experience of being unemployed?

Lyn: Well I wanted to do a course but you had to be unemployed for six months, and so I'm doing the hospitality course because I went in the day it was six months and said 'look, I want to do a course'. I mean basically I was just sick and tired of not knowing, like going down to the CES, looking through newspapers and trying to, like even door knocking to try and get a job. And it was just basically, I thought like I've just got to do something. I just don't want to do this for the rest of my life and I just thought if I did a course, like they say to do all these courses, but at least this had training in it as well, doing work experience and I thought that gives me hands on experience. And that's what they want these days.

And I thought 'well that's pretty good,' at least I can say I've had at least a bit of experience waitressing, like that's part of my hospitality course.

Lyn's comments indicate the improved sense of self-esteem that unemployed people often experience whilst participating in short term training courses. The short course provided Lyn with some skills and work experience that will probably improve her job prospects. However, the reason for her improved self-esteem is the changed form of the story that Lyn is able tell about her unemployment. This changed narrative is described as an imagined encounter, possibly with a prospective employer: 'And I thought 'well that's pretty good,' at least I can say I've had at least a bit of experience waitressing'. It is in this internalised imagined dialogue that understandings of unemployment are formed and transformed. Further, this dialogue is inextricably temporal: events in the past are interpreted in a narrative that changes anticipated prospects for the future. The experiences described in the strong romance job loss narratives represents the extension of this strategy to its limits. People who narrated their job loss as a strong romance saw their entire experience of unemployment, including their decision to leave their previous job, as a form of retraining that promised to lead into a new and highly desirable career.

Some people responded to the ongoing difficulty of finding employment by attempting to reduce the significance attached to working. This involved attempting to invest other identities with greater significance in order to reduce the importance of working. People used a variety of strategies to reduce the importance of working including developing a vigorous exercise program, visiting friends, and voluntary work. The important characteristic of these activities is not that they provide a 'functional' equivalent to working, as Jahoda (1982) suggests. Rather, it is that the person takes control of their life and invests it with a sense of purpose and worth independent of their status as an unemployed person. Bill, for example, recounted a period of unemployment after a tragic job loss two years previous to his current unemployment that provides an illustration of this process:

Bill: [The problem was that] I used to go to the local CES [Commonwealth Employment Service] every day, and if you got a job they'd say 'well we'll call you back at home'. So you'd go home waiting all day, each day for a phone call and you wouldn't get it. And that made me feel even worse ... So anyhow I just thought 'stuff this'. And so I'd go out and I'd do all my own stuff in the morning like running, swimming, go to the gym, and then around about 2.00 after I'd done what I wanted to do I'd go to the CES, go in and say 'anything happening? Are there any jobs?

Blah, blah, blah, nothing happening, OK, thanks very much, see you later'. I took control. The same with going [for interviews] for jobs, I'd go in and I'd say 'well look, can you give me a time [when you will ring me] because I'm pretty busy'. So I wasn't doing nothing with my life, just waiting to get a job. To get a job was not the most important thing to me. After a while I realised that my life, what I was doing, enjoying my life, living my life was more important than just getting a job.

When a person was able to 'take control' of their situation this enabled them to begin to experience a sense of agency and self-worth. Activities that would normally be secondary, such as exercising, visiting friends and voluntary work, were formed into life tasks that sustained a person's sense of self worth. Such a positive approach to unemployment is similar in some ways to those who understood unemployment as a holiday. In both cases the opportunities that being without work provide were celebrated and enjoyed. The important difference, however, is that Bill, and others who described similar positive periods, did not stop looking for work.

The ability to take a positive approach to unemployment is dependent on financial resources. Without the safety net provided by Social Security payments, unemployment would necessarily be a much more unpleasant experience. Even with these payments, debts incurred whilst employed meant that some people did not have enough money to survive. From this perspective it is difficult to be relaxed about looking for work. However, Charles' case demonstrates that even those who are financially secure find it difficult to make a positive response toward their unemployment.

Bill's attitude to his unemployment is a potentially difficult line to sustain because it is in some ways contradictory. Bill described himself as actively searching for work, which implies that finding employment was important to him. However, at the same time, he gave the activity of looking for work a secondary place in his priorities. 'Enjoying life' came first, and this included swimming, running, and various other activities. For most people in this study, working was typically the central life activity. All other activities revolved around it, including a person's ability to 'enjoy life'. Bill's relegation of work to a secondary position runs counter to most Western understandings of the meaning of work. This issue is discussed in greater detail in Chapter Eight.

Rob, whose experience was described in the previous Chapter, had also developed other activities that enabled him to sustain an active life-style whilst unemployed. He described the tensions and ambiguities that can arise as a consequence of reducing the importance a person attaches to working:

Rob: I want to work because I want to progress. I got a lot of things to do with money and I want to do things to the house which materials cost the money ... So I'm caught in this catch twenty-two situation. I'd love the time off and I could do a lot more with my time but I haven't got the money to buy materials to be doing a lot more with my time.

Rob had found considerable pleasure in his activities whilst unemployed and there were few incentives for him to work, although a higher income was attractive. When he was offered a job he struggled with the desire to turn it down because staying unemployed had become nearly as attractive as working. He finally decided he should take the job because 'you can't knock back a job when you are on unemployment [benefits]'. The attitude to unemployment described in the weak romantic job loss narratives forms the logical extension of this experience of unemployment. In the weak romance narratives, the search for employment was not an important issue. Other activities were considered much more important than working. This is consistent with Breakwell's (1984:493) observation that 'adjusting well' to unemployment, in the sense of not finding the transition stressful, was associated with a lower likelihood of getting a job.

People can be described as 'adapting' to unemployment in two main ways. Some people, such as Bill and Rob, continued to search for work at least periodically, but engaged in other activities whilst unemployed. These activities, the events of lived experience, were often developed out of a struggle to narrate unemployment in a less self-deprecating manner. Such activities enabled the person to sustain a narrative of self-identity with a modicum of self-esteem whilst they were unemployed. However, other people responded to the difficulty of finding work by passively resigning themselves to unemployment.

Tragic Unemployment: Depression and 'Fate'

Some tragic narratives of unemployment describe experiences of severe depression and self-deprecation. These experiences of depression can be either short lived, or more sustained. The strongest accounts are almost an inverse form of the strong romances. In these tragic narratives of unemployment the 'real self' that is discovered is devalued and worthless. This self-concept reaches back into the past, and forward into the future.

Vince's narrative provides one of the fullest and clearest accounts of this form of tragic unemployment.

When asked about his sacking Vince explained: 'I expected it. It's written in some contract somewhere that anyone that employs me can walk all over me and treat me like shit and sack me when they want'. Vince both blames himself and his 'fate'. The centrality of this explanation is demonstrated by Vince's response to the question 'Who am I?'

Doug: Can you give ten answers to the question 'who am I?' How would you try and answer that?

Vince: Who am I? You don't ask yourself that very often? I could say I'm not entirely sure, but I am. I'm another shit-kicker in society. I'm a fucked up individual who is, I hesitate to say a victim because, not a victim of society, but a victim of my upbringing.

Vince had constructed a narrative that emphasises his passivity in the face of a hostile world and a tragic fate. This narrative reaches back into his past and extends into his future. Stories about his upbringing, his early work experiences driving cabs at night, and his obsession with gambling, all emphasise his inability to control his life. While he knows he should have been able to control his gambling problems, he was not able to, and this is representative of how he sees himself. Similarly, Vince feels that he is unable to control his future. Unlike Diana and Geoff's strong romance narratives, Vince is not doing anything that suggests his dreams to become a fishing guide and sell fishing bait for a living might become a reality. He himself says of his story about working as a fishing guide: 'Anyway, that's another dream'.

Other studies have described similar tragic narratives where people attempt to explain activities that seem out of character or morally questionable. Langer (1991:176) suggests that the 'interaction of self with destiny has been a hallmark of tragic literature since its inception'. One of the holocaust survivors quoted by Langer (1991:176) attempts to explain her seemingly inexplicable actions in the concentration camps saying: 'my fate push me, you know. I not help myself'. Likewise, Modell (1992) describes how the metaphor of coercion is central to the narratives of birthparents who relinquished their children for adoption: 'Relinquish, give up, give away, surrender: none conveyed a positive action, and all suggested an unwilling decision: "I had no choice"' (Modell 1992:80). Coercion explained the paradox between the typically valued event of having a child, that at the same time was a moment of denying parental status through the act of relinquishing that child.

Similarly, Vince makes sense of his experience in terms of 'a contract' that says he will be treated 'like shit'. In Vince's account, identity is forced upon him by circumstances and this explains why he is still unemployed. Romantic job loss narratives describe active interventions in the world to shape and control the person's circumstances. These actions are justified by an appeal to general values such as creativity and self-control. In contrast, in tragic narratives of unemployment, while the protagonist sometimes appears to be the author of his or her own activity, 'spectator and chorus alike know that the narrative itself will eventually overwhelm the character in such a manner that she [or he] must succumb to the inevitable unfolding of events' (Rasmussen 1995:165). Rather than actively controlling the events of his life, Vince's narrative emphasises his passivity in the face of forces that he cannot control or resist. His inactivity is justified by an appeal to this narrative.

The social sources of this form of explanation are clear in Vince's account. When I asked Vince what his friends thought about his sacking he said that they all thought it was 'par for the course, they know what the employment situation is like'. These friends are typically in a similar situation to Vince, either unemployed or working in insecure jobs. Vince reported that an official representative of the Commonwealth Employment Service had also discouraged him from 'wasting his time' looking too hard for work because he was unlikely to be successful. The important point is not whether this is an 'accurate' reflection of Vince's actual job prospects or an 'accurate' account of what other people have said to him. Rather, the point is that this is what Vince understands to be the case. Social psychological research (Rosenberg 1979) has demonstrated that people's self-evaluations typically correspond with what they think other people think about them, rather than with what other people actually report thinking about them. From Vince's point of view there is little point in trying to do anything to find a job, because he will inevitably fail, and he understands his close friends to agree with him on this point.

It could be suggested that Vince is deceiving himself when he describes his unemployment as his fate. Similarly, Modell suggests that the metaphor of coercion utilised by birthparents who relinquished their children for adoption is self-deceptive because of the way the narrative was learnt through meetings and newsletters (Rosenwald and Ochberg 1992:10-11). Modell's argument seems to be that because the narrative form is derived intersubjectively, there must therefore be a disparity between the story as told and the story as it was actually lived. However, narratives are not self-deceptive simply because they are derived from intersubjective sources. This would make all narratives acts of self-deception. Polonoff

(1987) describes a more sophisticated understanding of self-deception in terms of the internal and external coherence of the self-narrative and its 'livability'. From this perspective the problematic nature of tragic unemployment narratives lies in the implications for how a person lives their life, and in the consistency, or inconsistency, of the narrative with the attitudes of close friends and other influential people in the person's life. On at least two out of three of these points Vince's narrative is unsatisfactory and potentially self-deceptive. As will be described shortly Vince was clearly not enjoying his current lifestyle, and some of his close friends, particularly his spouse, did not accept his line about unemployment being his fate. However, Vince's narrative did not lack internal coherence.

Tragic narratives of unemployment were typically internally coherent. The most recent job loss was described as part of a longer narrative that reached back into the person's early biography and forward into their expectations about the future. The narratives cover a long time frame in which the episodes support the general theme that the person is a 'victim' or unable to control their destiny. Tragic unemployment narratives describe unemployment as more than a temporary hiatus in the person's career. Rather, the last job appears as the temporary hiatus. Unemployment activates a self-narrative that emphasises the person's inability to achieve or be successful. This narrative reaches into both the past and the future suggesting that fate has decreed the person will never be successful. The low self-worth implied in this narrative is difficult to combat because of the strongly coherent form of the narrative. Further, it also has an impact on the person's actions. 'For instance, actions that require a self-presentation as competent or confident are difficult to negotiate when behavior is mediated by a working self-concept that features the 'unsuccessful professional' possible self as a focal point' (Markus and Nurius 1986:962).

In Vince's case, his resignation in the face of a tragic fate, combined with an extended liminal period of unemployment led to extremes of depression and suicidal thoughts:

Doug: You said that unemployment was OK at first, but it gets to you after a while.

Vince: Yeah, you can be on the dole for so long and you know you have plenty of time to yourself and you don't have money but at least you've got time to yourself and that's very over-rated. You can have too much time to yourself and when you do, when you start watching the day time soaps and getting involved in them, or when you've got too much time to think, when you've been doing it for too long, then you start climbing the

walls looking for jobs because you've been unemployed too long, you
haven't had a solid work history, ever, which gets you down. You start
thinking of offing yourself [suicide] as... I mean, I've been that close to
offing myself so many times that you lose count and it's just purely the
fact that I'm too gutless to do it is why I haven't done it. Because there's
no reason for my existence. I oppose existence in every way shape and
form, I shouldn't be here, I know I shouldn't be here, there's no reason for
me to be here at all. I'm not contributing anything to the human race.
I'm not contributing anything to the planet except maybe shit. So there's
no reason for me to be here.

Unemployed people commonly emphasise the need to feel needed;
and unemployment suggests that a person is not needed by society.
Vince's suicidal thoughts are explained as an extension of the implication
that he has no value to society. Further, it is in a coherent narrative
about his tragic fate that Vince makes sense of his apparent worthlessness
to society.

Vince's claim, quoted above, that 'I oppose existence in every way
shape and form' is another form of Ricoeur's paradoxical sentence 'I am
nothing'. As I noted in Chapter Three, Ricoeur argues that the paradoxical
form of this sentence must be retained because 'nothing' would be
meaningless if it were not imputed to an 'I'. 'What is still "I" when I say
that it is nothing if not precisely a self deprived of assistance from
sameness?' (Ricoeur 1992:166). While Vince's tragic narrative does
provide him with some sense of continuity with the past, this continuity
is dissatisfying or discordant in the sense that it is an ongoing experience
of being worthless and powerless. The liminality of unemployment has
become central to Vince's narrative. He defines himself in negative
terms: having no valued place in society, not being in control, not being
able to contribute anything of worth.

Langer (1991) describes a similar experience amongst holocaust
survivors, although of a much more extreme and protracted nature.
Holocaust testimonies articulate what it means to live without a sense of
agency, where choices are withdrawn and moral frameworks have to be
discarded. According to the vocabulary of moral philosophy (Taylor
1989; MacIntyre 1981) lives take on meaning, a sense of worth and
progression when they are articulated in narratives that emphasise agency,
utilise clear moral frameworks, and are oriented toward a moral community.
This seems to imply that narratives describing a damaged personhood
without agency, choice, or morals are in some way not properly human.
However, Langer argues that the disintegrative testimonies of holocaust
survivors, and the damaged personhood that they describe, is not simply
a product of a failure to narrate their experiences adequately.

Disintegrative narratives that do not describe a unified heroic identity are not necessarily invalid or illegitimate. Rather, the holocaust testimonies represent the 'reality' of the disintegrative milieu of their lived experience that is a 'communal wound that cannot heal' (Langer 1991:204). Narratives of anguish that present a damaged, diminished self are just as legitimate as heroic narratives.

The liminal experiences of the unemployed are a far cry from the experiences of holocaust survivors. To begin with, the narratives of unemployment typically posses a clearer plot, even if it is tragic. The holocaust testimonies that Langer (1991) describes are plotless. However, there is an important parallel. In both cases people describe a deep discontinuity or, to use Ricoeur's phrase, a discordance that threatens the integrity of the self and disrupts the continuity of the self-narrative. Being without work deprives the person of their sense of sameness, and is inconsistent with central commitments they have made to other people and to themselves. Despite all their attempts the person remains in a non-status: unemployed. It is therefore not surprising that Charles finds it hard to talk about how he felt during this time, or that Vince has contemplated suicide.

The Multiple Possibilities of Narrative Form

White (1973:9) suggests that tragedies are not completely destructive stories for those who survive them. For both the spectators and the protagonist there has been a 'gain in consciousness'. At the time of his interview Charles was leaving the liminal phase and beginning a reintegrative phase into a new job that he had just been offered. Charles observed: 'And yeah once you have the job, you feel that the whole process has been worthwhile, and I felt that I grew through that whole process'. From his perspective of having gained a new job, Charles could also say:

Charles: Now, you know, I suppose, having got this job, I'm having regrets now perhaps, that perhaps I didn't take three or four months out, and just go on an overseas trip, be unemployed, and see the world. Live a lot of different life's experiences. I suddenly realise now that that opportunity is no longer available to me. So long as I work I've only got four weeks a year leave. So in some ways I missed an opportunity there through this feeling that I had to get a job.

In other words, Charles now realises that there were other ways he could have narrated his job loss and subsequent unemployment and other ways he could, therefore, have acted. He specifically mentions a narrative that has the structure of a weak romance. Charles' financial resources may have enabled him to successfully employ this narrative strategy and this may have led to a more pleasant experience for him. In contrast, Vince did not have Charles' resources and while he did begin his unemployment claiming to enjoy the free time, the absence of money meant that this claim was not sustainable for very long. Vince, it could be said, appears to have begun his unemployment using a particularly weak romance narrative that quickly disintegrated into a tragedy.

Lived experience does not determine the form of a narrative. However, neither are people free to narrate their experiences in whatever way they choose. The enduring nature of a person's past self-narratives, the influence of cultural repertoires, and the constraints imposed by previous decisions all shape a person's experience and the form of their narrative of that experience. Vince's narrative cannot simply be reshaped independent of the events of his lived experience. While some of the events of Vince's lived experience are open to change through his own choice, other aspects are reflections of the power of more general social processes. The casualization of the labour force and the consumerist culture of modern society are two examples of more general social processes that shape both the events of Vince's life, and the narrative that he uses to interpret and respond to these events.

Conclusion

This Chapter has argued that depression and low self-esteem experienced during unemployment are a product of the way the experience is understood. After a tragic job loss people enter a liminal stage in which relationships and narratives that previously sustained a sense of self-identity are further disturbed. Searching for a new job is the main response to this liminal experience. However, people also use other strategies to minimise the threat to their identity, such as reducing the importance they attach to their work identity. The experience of unemployment changes over time, as do the narratives used to interpret this experience. Minimally it is clear that people experience periods in which they are more positive and hopeful about their future, and periods in which they are more despairing. Periods of severe depression are associated with narratives that emphasise the person's passivity in the face of a tragic fate.

Finally, I have argued that the form of the narrative used to interpret job loss and unemployment is neither determined by the events of lived experience, nor is the narrative independently free to take any shape or form. Rather, people develop interpretations of their experience in a complex ongoing process where events and narrative interpretations are mutually influential. While there is some freedom to choose the form of their stories, this freedom is constrained by past choices and larger social structural forces.

7 Complex Job Loss

Introduction

For some people being a worker is absolutely central to their self-understanding, while for others it may be almost irrelevant, with another role such as being a parent, at the centre of their self-understanding. Symbolic interactionists pointed out some time ago that identities vary in salience or centrality (Kuhn and McPartland 1954; McCall and Simmons 1966; Turner 1972; Rosenberg 1979). McCall and Simmons (1966:77-78) identify several determinants of the centrality of an identity. These include the person's subjective sense of the importance of the identity; support from relevant other people for the identity; the degree of commitment to the identity; the extent that a person's planned future is predicated on the identity; and intrinsic and extrinsic rewards gained from maintenance of the identity. In short, the structure of self-understanding and the structure of a person's lived experience are integrally related. However, this concept of identity salience is atemporal. I have argued for temporal conceptions of identity as narrative-identity, and lived experience as status passage. Narrative-identities and status passages also vary in centrality or salience.

Glaser and Strauss (1971:144) observed that at any one time people are usually going through more than one status passage. Any particular transition is only one of a number of concurrent passages that make up the totality of a person's experience. Similarly, the narrative-identity formed and transformed through any particular status passage is only one of a number of concurrent narrative-identities that make up the totality of the person's self-narratives. In other words, the self-narrative is not a monologue, but rather can be conceptualised as polyphonic (Hermans et al. 1993). Some narratives are more central to a person's self-story, whilst others are more peripheral. The centrality of any particular identity changes through time as the self-narrative is created and recreated in response to the events, or passages, of lived experience. This Chapter describes precisely these sorts of changes to the centrality of the work identity.

Rosenberg (1979) argued that the more central an identity, the greater its effect on 'global' self-evaluations. Global self-evaluations relate to the self as a whole as opposed to evaluations of one particular identity. Studies of status passages support this hypothesised relationship between identity centrality and consequences for global self-esteem. For

112

example, the extent of grief experienced by a bereaved person reflects the nature of the relationship between the subject and the deceased. The closer the ties, the more prolonged and traumatising is the grief response (Parkes 1985). Similarly, Parsons (1951:443) observed that the extent of 'emotional shock', frustration and anxiety associated with an illness is closely related to the severity of the illness - in other words, the more central the illness, the greater its impact. Applying this point to the experience of job loss suggests that the more central the work identity, the greater the impact of job loss on global self-evaluations.

In previous Chapters the analysis focused on narratives in which job loss was the central status passage that influenced a person's self-evaluations. While there were other concurrent passages, these were secondary to, and subsumed by, the events of the job loss. However, job loss is not always the most important influence on a person's self-understanding.

I use the term complex job loss to refer to narratives in which the meaning of the job loss is complicated by events in non-work roles. Complex job loss narratives describe a second major status passage that occurs concurrently with the job loss. Seven of the interviewees indicated that other events in their lives were at least as important as the consequences of their job loss. Two people were negotiating a marriage separation at the time of their job loss, two others had chronic illnesses, one person was having a 'faith crisis,' two people left work in order to move cities, one to be with his 'true love' and the other to be free of some extremely problematic 'friends'. I will refer to this disparate group of non-work related transitions as complicating passages.

The job loss passage was primarily understood or evaluated in terms of its effect on the complicating passage. Five people saw their job loss as positive because it provided them with time and resources to deal with problems created by the complicating passage. On the other hand, two people saw the job loss as adding to the stress of their situation. I will refer to these, respectively, as complex romantic job loss narratives and complex tragic job loss narratives, and the remainder or this Chapter discusses in detail each narrative form in that order. I conclude with a short discussion of the relationship between complex narratives and the concept of 'employment commitment' commonly used in the unemployment literature.

Complex Romantic Job Loss

Complex romances describe job loss as a positive transition, at least initially. However, unlike the 'uncomplicated' romantic job loss narratives described in Chapter Four, unemployment was not viewed primarily as an opportunity to work toward a new occupation or to go on a holiday. Rather, job loss was positive because it provided the opportunity to use the person's time and resources to solve problems associated with a complicating passage. The events in the complicating passage were central to the person's self-identity, and the narrative about these events was romantic in form. The breakdown of a marriage, for example, caused severe distress for the person, and their job loss provided the opportunity to attempt to alleviate this distress and work toward an improved future. Job loss is neither irrelevant to the person's self-narrative, nor is it the dominant influence. Job loss plays a secondary role as a significant influence on the main narrative of the complicating passage.

There were two primary reasons for being pleased with finishing work. First, three people needed time out from employment in order to recover from the distress of separation, or to regain their health after a serious illness. Second, two people wanted to move to a different location. Once they had moved, they immediately began to look for a new job. In both cases, the resolution of the problems associated with the complicating passage resulted in the declining salience or centrality of the complicating passage as an influence on the person's life as a whole. Being without work began to become more problematic and central to the person's self-narrative. The narratives used to describe the problem of liminality during unemployment then began to resemble the 'uncomplicated' romantic and tragic narratives of job loss described in previous Chapters. One person had begun to attempt to retrain himself for a new career, explaining his experience in a narrative similar in form to the strong romance narratives of job loss. The other four people's narratives of unemployment were closer to accounts of liminality in the tragic job loss narratives. They described similar experiences of desperately wanting work, but being unable to obtain employment.

Figure 7 provides a graphic image of the most common form of a complex romance. Prior to the job loss, both work and the complicating passage caused considerable distress. However, the distress caused by the complicating passage was considered more important. Immediately after the job loss, being unemployed was not a strong influence on global self-evaluations. As the complicating passage takes its course, it becomes less distressing, and may even be the basis of some feelings of pride and self-confidence. On the other hand, as the problems of the complicating passage recede, the experience of unemployment becomes increasingly distressing.

Figure 7 Complex romantic job loss narratives

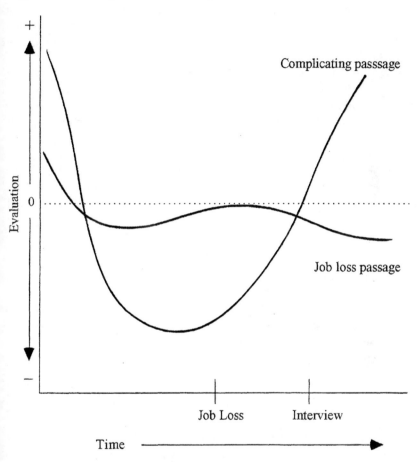

Romantic job loss narratives, described in Chapter Four, all began by describing their last job as oppressive or unpleasant. Similarly, in the complex romances three people also described their last job as oppressive and this added to the distress caused by the complicating passage. Their narratives could be described as 'doubly romantic' because they hoped that the job loss would not only solve the problems of the complicating passage, but also enable them to find a new, more satisfying occupation.

However, because the main influence on their self-narrative was the complicating passage, a negative evaluation of the last job was not essential for the narrative to have the form of a complex romance. One person was ambivalent about their last job, and another had derived great pleasure from their last job. Both these people still thought that leaving their last job was a positive move, and after a period of change to deal with the problems of the complicating passage, expected the future to lead to an improved quality of life.

Kylie was thirty years old when I interviewed her and had been unemployed for twelve months. Her last job had been as a salesperson for a large clothing store chain. She had worked with the company for about twelve years and had become increasingly frustrated with the difficult conditions under which she was expected to work. During the recession in the early 1990s they had laid off staff and this meant that Kylie frequently worked alone for long hours, often without breaks. However, the main cause of distress at the time of her job loss was her separation after the breakdown of her marriage. Kylie had begun to see a therapist to help her deal with her separation, and the therapist initially suggested taking some time off work:

Doug: So you took 6 weeks off and went overseas. What happened after that?
Kylie: I went back to work two days after coming back and I think having been
         away and come back to a marriage break-down and the conditions I was
         working in was just all too much. And I was this far away from a nervous
         break-down and that's when I went back to my therapist and she said that
         I shouldn't have even been at work the way I was looking and feeling I
         guess ...
Doug: So, what happened in the few months before you actually left?
Kylie: Well, I just made a decision. In fact my counsellor sort of prompted me
         to make the decision because she knew I didn't like the job, she knew that
         the conditions weren't any good, and she believes, believed that there were
         plenty of [pause]. My thoughts were I can't leave because I'm separated
         and what do I do without a job and things like that, and she suggested
         that peace of mind and getting myself together was more important than
         having the 320 dollars as opposed to the hundred and whatever dollars
         that you get on the social security. So I just made that decision and
         thought: 'I've got to do what's best for me'.
Doug: And you think that was a right decision?
Kylie: Oh absolutely.

In Kylie's account the rewards of employment are explicitly identified as secondary. Leaving her job was a way of reducing her stress levels so she could sort out her main problem: the consequences of her separation.

Similar to the romantic job loss narratives Kylie's dramatisation of her thoughts emphasises her agency and control over her situation. Further, the intersubjective sources of Kylie's decision and narrative interpretation are clearly illustrated in the dialogue with her therapist.

Kylie's interpretation of her unemployment appears to have changed at least twice. Initially leaving work was feared, because she thought: 'what can I do without a job'. However, her therapist convinced her that peace of mind was more important than security of income. Unemployment was therefore welcomed as an opportunity to sort out her problems. She was further encouraged to leave her job because she believed that there were plenty of jobs available. However, once she sorted out many of the problems associated with her separation, being without work became increasingly onerous, compounded by the discovery that employment was much harder to find than at first thought. The change in tense in the sentence: 'she [the therapist] believes, believed that there were plenty of [pause]' with the implied ending 'plenty of jobs,' suggests that her therapist has also shared this last change in interpretation of unemployment.

For Kylie, the particular job and the work identity associated with it were temporarily surrendered in order to enable her to solve serious problems associated with other central aspects of the self. Kylie feared a complete mental breakdown if she continued to work. Charmaz (1994:278) describes a similar strategy amongst chronically ill men who relinquish some identities in order to preserve others. However, complex romances do not involve the permanent abandonment of an identity. Kylie, and the four other people in this category, anticipated that they would at some stage begin to work again. Career considerations temporarily took a second place in order to enable them to resolve the issues and problems associated with the complicating passage. This points to the dynamic and 'in process' nature of the self and narrated identities. The narratives that constitute self-identity are not fixed, but change in response to the variety of events that make up a person's life. Some narrative-identities are more central than others, but the centrality of these identities changes in response to the passages of lived experience.

Complex Tragic Job Loss

Complex tragedies describe the events of the job loss as adding to the distress the person was already experiencing as a consequence of the complicating passage. Two people's narratives had the form of a complex tragedy. The complicating passages involved a 'loss of faith' and a serious illness. The main problem that the person faced was the tragic loss of an imagined future as a consequence of the complicating passage. Similar to the tragic job loss narratives described in Chapter Five, the 'loss of faith' and the serious illness had destroyed plans for the future, leaving the person feeling excluded from society and bereft of any sense that the future might bring an improvement to their problems.

Figure 8   Complex tragic job loss narratives

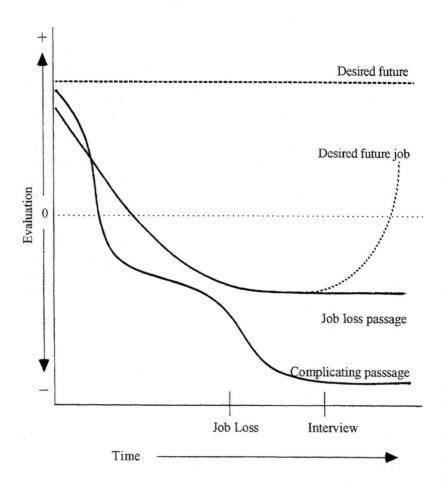

In both cases being without work reinforced the sense of isolation and worthlessness already present as a consequence of the tragic complicating passage. One person was pleased to leave her last job, whilst the other person was more satisfied with his last job. Both people, however, were not pleased to be without work. They hoped that they would be able to sort out some of their problems in the future when they found another job. In contrast to complex romances where job loss provided a solution to current problems, complex tragedies described unemployment as contributing to current problems.

Figure 8 represents the complex tragedies graphically. Beginning at the top of the figure, at some stage in the past the person had a positively valued imagined future as a missionary, or of being able-bodied. This imagined future is now clearly impossible, or at least highly unlikely. The person, however, still has to deal with commitments and relationships that were premised on this imagined future. Second, while there were some unpleasant aspects to the last job, being unemployed is more distressing. With the fading of the earlier imagined future, a future job now holds out some hope for an improvement in their situation. However, finding a new job will not solve all the problems created by the complicating passage. Past commitments and actions associated with the complicating passage will continue to cause significant distress if they cannot be resolved. Both the job loss and the complicating passage are tragic. Both describe an unattained desired future, and a present status that is undesirable and distressing.

Judy was thirty-one years old when I interviewed her. After completing a Bachelor of Arts she trained for several years to become a missionary. She had subsequently worked overseas as a missionary for a year, and returned to Australia to work in the central office of her missionary society. However, Judy had begun to question her faith: 'and so having come to this point where I am really not sure what the right values for life are any more and I am not really sure how to understand how God acts in my life and that sort of stuff'. From this perspective missionary service overseas was no longer a desirable plan for her future. At the centre of Judy's distress was the loss or destruction of a life plan in which she had invested most of her resources.

Four months prior to her interview Judy had finished her work at the Missionary Society by mutual agreement. She recognised that she could no longer work there, and they could not afford to pay her unless she resumed her work overseas as a missionary. While being unable to find work was a major problem for Judy, her 'faith crisis' was the broader picture that framed her current trauma and distress. The loss of the anticipated future as a person who 'believed in God' was the primary source of her tragic narrative. Finding secular employment was a fall back position, a secondary imagined future that was also unattained, and this secondary loss reinforced the tragic form of her narrative.

Judy's sense of being unwanted and isolated was attributed to both her 'faith crisis' and her unemployment. She attempted to explain her problems to some of her Christian friends, but they 'sort of gave me nice [intended ironically] pat answers'. The attitudes of these Christians friends made Judy feel extremely uncomfortable and she had 'put some distance' between herself and them. A more generalised sense of being unwanted was crystalized in a seemingly trivial, but nonetheless symbolic shopping expedition where Judy was unable to find shoes that would fit her long slim feet. '[I] began to think: This society doesn't want me. There isn't a place for me in this society. And that has just perpetuated my belief that the way to protect myself is to withdraw'. The dramatisation of these thoughts underlines the described loss of worth. The inability to find work reinforced a more general feeling of being lost and unwanted.

Doug: Thinking now about the future.
Judy: Is there any? Does there have to be a future? [Laughs] ...
Doug: So what is your sense of the future then?
Judy: Ask Bruce [her partner].
Doug: No, I am asking you.
Judy: You see, I'm trying, I'm sort of not really thinking about it.

Judy is in a liminal phase for both her passages concurrently. She is uncertain about how to deal with the loss of her faith and she is uncertain about the sort of job for which she should apply. Fearing that she will remain in this liminal state, she tries to avoid thinking about the future, which only looks bleak.

Most of Judy's relationships, including her marriage, were premised on her identity as a missionary. She had recently married, and her partner had given up his permanent job to go to Bible college for a year so that they could both go overseas as missionaries. Judy's life to this point had been so focused on becoming a missionary that she could not imagine an alternative desirable future. Charmaz observed a similar effect in her study of chronically ill men: 'if they could define no valued realm of action available to them and no way to preserve a valued self, the likelihood that they would slip into depression increased' (Charmaz 1994:284). While Judy had enquired about a number of courses and a few jobs, these had all provided negative responses. Consistent with the analysis of the rejection of job applications in Chapter Seven, these experiences reinforced Judy's sense of worthlessness.

Ball (1976) and Harris' (1978) discussions of failure in sporting careers describe a similar passage where the person had invested almost everything in a particular career. High levels of distress are experienced by athletes who had intended to reach the apex of athletic success and left no alternatives to that aspiration. The more central the lost role is to a person's life plan, the greater the impact of failure in that role. Distress and lowered self-esteem can be seen as a kind of disappointment. That is to say, divestment passages may result in a 'disappointment of goals to which a person is implicitly committed and by which that person has defined her or his own worth' (Oatley and Bolton 1985:375).

Other people, such as Charles (Chapter Five) described a similarly high level of investment in secular careers. However, Judy's experience is different because her problem is more complex than simply a desire to change careers. Judy is attempting to leave a religious vocation and enter a secular career. This transition involves two concurrent passages, one associated with her religious world view, and the other with employment. Her sense of worthlessness derives from the loss of faith in a world view that gave her life and relationships coherence and meaning. While finding another job will solve some of her more pressing problems, including financial concerns and a lack of structure to her day, she will still have to resolve the implications of her 'faith crisis' for her world view, her marriage, and other important relationships.

Complex Job Loss Narratives and Self-Evaluations

In this Chapter I have argued that the relationship of the work identity to other aspects of a person's life must be taken into account in any attempt to explain the variable consequences of unemployment. Atchley (1976:22) makes a similar observation with respect to retirement. He points out that many professionals, including sociologists, hold a romanticised view of work, assuming that the job is always a central focus of those people who have employment. However the functions and meaning of employment vary considerably depending on the relationship of work to other life spheres. It cannot be simply assumed that retirement, or unemployment, must necessarily be the most significant influence on a person's self understanding.

In the unemployment literature there has been some research into the effect of 'employment commitment' or the 'Protestant Ethic' as a moderating variable (see for example Jackson et al. 1983; Rowley and Feather 1987). The findings of these studies are consistent with the above analysis: greater commitment to the work role is correlated with a greater impact of unemployment on the individual. However, these studies of employment commitment are narrowly conceived.

It is an over simplification to describe a work identity as more or less central to a reified atemporal self-concept. Rather, people experience multiple status passages concurrently, and the interpretation of these passages in a narrative-identity is developed within the broader perspective of all ongoing transitions. This means that changes in other life passages can influence the interpretation of the job loss passage. Kylie, for example, described the way in which leaving work had initially been attractive because she needed time and energy to deal with her marriage breakdown. However, after she had come through those difficulties, unemployment took on a new significance, becoming a problem rather than a solution. This Chapter has demonstrated it should not be assumed that because a person is distressed, or elated, after losing a job that the cause of their problems, or joy, lies in their unemployed status. In this sample, seven of the thirty-eight job losses examined clearly identified events in non-work roles as the dominant influence on their self-evaluations.

8 Unemployment and the Meaning of Working

Introduction

Responses to unemployment cannot be adequately interpreted without a sophisticated understanding of the meaning of working. Job loss is like a breaching experiment (Garfinkel 1967). The experience of being without work exposes the meaning of working in a different light. This Chapter examines explicitly on the relationship between the experience of unemployment and the meaning of working.

Chapters Four to Seven examined the experience of job loss leading into unemployment emphasising the relationship between the events of lived experience and their interpretation in a narrative. The present Chapter examines the relationship between narrative-identities and cultural discourses. Cultural discourses are also variously termed preexisting narratives, sedimented traditions, cultural repertoires, discourses of power, and stereotypes. The experience of job loss provides an important perspective on the link between an individual's narrative-identity and more general cultural discourses about the meaning of working.

The Chapter begins with a discussion of labour process theory and management theory. This literature examines the social construction of the meaning of working, focusing on the influence of more general cultural discourses. The Chapter then reviews some interview materials that explore the relationship between cultural discourses and self-narratives. Specifically I examine the expectation that a person should work in order to be an adult member of society and the variations in this expectation for men and women. This section demonstrates that cultural discourses are not passively accepted, but are also used and manipulated by individuals. Further, similar to the influence of cultural discourses on individual narratives, changes to the organisation of society shape the events of an individual's lived experience. Specifically, some of the problems experienced by unemployed people are a consequence of the changing organisation of work where permanent jobs are becoming increasingly difficult to obtain. Finally, the role of agency in unemployment narratives is discussed. This takes the analysis of the relationship between the society and the individual through the full circle. Cultural discourses and social structural changes shape the stories people tell about unemployment. However, these stories are not determined by events and cultural resources - the individual's skill as a story teller also shapes their experience of unemployment. However, even this is not as simple as it seems, because some individuals have more resources, both financial and cultural, than others, and the level of resources shapes the opportunity to tell good stories about the experience of unemployment.

The Labour Process

Since Braverman (1974) published *Labour and Monopoly Capitalism*, sociological investigations of work have tended to focus on the organisation of the work task in the workplace, also referred to as the 'labour process'. Braverman restated Marx's initial analysis of the oppression of workers. Specifically he examined management's attempt to increase control over the work process, particularly through Tayloristic work practices. As a consequence of Braverman's emphasis on the 'objective' organisation of the workplace, worker's subjective experiences of working have been largely ignored in the labour process literature. Most subsequent analysts of the labour process have followed Braverman's lead by explicitly ignoring the subjective experience of workers. While the critics of this omission are numerous (Cutler 1978; Littler and Salaman 1982), there have been relatively few attempts to develop a sophisticated theory of subjectivity in the labour process literature (Ezzy 1997). Thompson has suggested: 'the construction of a full theory of the missing subject is probably the greatest task facing labour process theory' (quoted in Willmott 1990:335).

In response to Braverman's (1974) neglect of subjectivity some of his critics have outlined how workers are involved in class struggles and negotiations. However, 'reducing the subjective dimension to an analysis of labour resistance, however valuable in its own right, has the unintended effect of replacing Braverman's determinism with a control-resistance dualism or paradigm' (Knights 1990:305). These critics tend to draw on a humanistic Marxist framework that represents subjectivity as the autonomous and creative aspects of human life. In other words, the labour process literature suffers from a similar problem to the unemployment literature, the person is either depicted as a passive reflection of social structure, or as an active autonomous subject resisting the influence of oppressive social forces.

A conception of the self as constructed through narrative provides a conception of subjectivity that mediates structure and agency. As argued in Chapter Three, the self is neither a solitary entity impervious to the influence of others, nor is it a mere reflection of objective structures. Rather, in the process of self-interpretation a person uses socially learnt cultural discourses to construct and reconstruct a coherent sense of self.

Outside of the labour process literature there have been a number of investigations of the experience of the worker at work, particularly by psychologists and management theorists. In a review of this literature Rose (1989) observes that during the second half of the twentieth century there has been a significant change in management theory's understanding of the worker. In the early part of the century thinkers such as Frederick Taylor (1913) and Henry Ford (1923) assumed that most workers preferred mindless labour. Ford argued that managers should control the organisation of work and that most workers were 'dumb', 'stupid', and should be treated like 'animals': 'To them the ideal job is one where the creative instinct need not be expressed' (Ford 1923:102). In the first part of the century a worker's creativity and self-conception were ignored. In contrast, during the second part of the century 'the management of subjectivity has become a central task for the modern organization' (Rose 1989:2). Whyte (1956) was an early observer of this change in management's understanding of workers. While a manager utilising old authoritarian forms of control was terrifying in some respects 'at least it could be said of him that what he wanted primarily from you was your sweat. The new man wants your soul' (Whyte 1956:397). The older, instrumental forms of control used financial rewards and threats to elicit compliance with rules and regulations. Kriegler (1980), for example, describes the way in which hire-purchase loans ensured the commitment of the labourers at the BHP shipyards in Whyalla, South Australia. In contrast, the newer form of management uses normative control. 'Normative control is the attempt to elicit and direct the required efforts of members by controlling the underlying experiences, thoughts, and feelings that guide their actions' (Kunda 1992:11). In this form of organisation the worker's self-conception becomes an object of management control.

Normative methods of control in the work place are consistent with the broader emphasis on the self as a consumer rather than a producer in the late twentieth century (Rose 1989:102). As the market becomes increasingly central to modern social organisation, the activities by which a person defines themselves are increasingly related to consumption rather than production. Further, market oriented consumerist culture emphasises the individual's freedom to choose and construct their own life-style. From the plethora of products and services available a person selects and constructs the content of their own self-concept. This emphasis on constructing oneself is reflected in the experience of working:

The image of the citizen as a choosing self entails a new image of the productive subject. The worker is portrayed neither as an economic actor, rationally pursuing financial advantage, nor as a social creature seeking satisfaction of needs for solidarity and security. The worker is an individual in search of meaning, responsibility, a sense of personal achievement, a maximized 'quality of life', and hence of work. Thus the individual is not to be emancipated *from* work, perceived as merely a task or a means to an end, but to be fulfilled *in* work, now construed as an activity through which we produce, discover, and experience our selves. (Rose 1989:103, original emphasis)

In other words, the meaning of working has been undergoing a major transition. In the past the ideals of the worker were in direct conflict with those of management. As McDonald (1994:37) puts it: labour's 'persistent affirmation of the morality and the dignity of the work, [was] opposed to the employer's attempt to strip work of its creativity and meaning'. Alternatively instrumental orientations saw work as a means of financing fulfilment in leisure or family relationships outside of the work role (Goldthorpe et al. 1978). However, in the new forms of work organisation both management and the worker want the worker to find fulfilment in the job. Self-understandings are both discovered and developed at work as a 'raw material' of the system (McDonald 1994:40).

Grey (1994) provides a clear illustration of this more recent form of work organisation in his account of the pursuit of a 'career' as a form of self-discipline amongst accountants. Grey describes how accountants devote themselves to their career. This devotion is performed willingly because self-fulfilment is found, or anticipated, at work, in the career, rather than elsewhere. The career becomes integral to the self and is viewed as a project. Extra-curricula responsibilities at university, social-networks, and even a person's marriage partner, are chosen, suggests Grey, with an eye to maximising the chance of career success.

Grey (1994:481) draws on a Foucauldian framework in his analysis of the 'self-disciplined project of self-management through career', emphasising 'how career, as part of the project of the self, can constitute labour process discipline and surveillance'. Newton (1996) suggests two problems with Grey's analysis. First, while Grey correctly points to the social constitution of subjectivity, in the Foucauldian framework the person is presented as an almost passive product of the various discourses of power. A more sophisticated understanding must go beyond a passive conception of the person as a mere reflection of discourses: 'there nevertheless remains a need to explain how subjects relate to and 'manoeuvre' around discourse' (Newton 1996:139). Second, the social sources of career discourses go largely unexplored. Newton picks up this second point, developing on the work of Elias to analyse the social sources of discourses by examining parallels between medieval courtly practices described by Elias and the social practices of accountants.

The Foucauldian analysis of technologies of subjectivity and discourses of power privileges these social forces over and against the person's response to them. According to de Certeau (1984:xii) Foucault focuses on the process of production, at the expense of an analysis of consumption. In contrast, de Certeau points, for example, to what the indigenous American Indians did with the Spanish religion that was imposed upon them. Specific rituals were made to take on meanings quite different to those intended by the Spanish. More generally he points to the way in which 'users make (*bricolent*) innumerable and infinitesimal transformations of and within the dominant cultural economy in order to adapt it to their own interests and their own rules' (de Certeau 1984:xiv). In the same way cultural discourses about careers and work are variously accepted, resisted, and transformed in people's day to day lives.

Kunda's (1992) analysis of culture in 'Hi Tech's' electronic engineering section makes precisely this point with respect to working 'culture' at Hi Tech. Kunda describes the company's use of normative control through an emphasis on company 'culture'. Employees are encouraged to internalise the company's goals and values and develop a strong emotional attachment to the organisation. As a consequence the bureaucratic forms of control, relying on financial threats and rewards are unnecessary. 'Instead productive work is the result of a combination of self-direction, initiative, and emotional attachment, and ultimately combines the organisational interest in productivity with the employees' personal interest in growth and maturity' (Kunda 1992:10). In other words the employees of 'Hi Tech' are committed to the company's 'culture' in the same way that the accountants studied by Grey (1994) are committed to accountancy culture, embodied in the idea of a 'career'.

However, Kunda points out that normative control is not unquestioned. Rather, there are many hints of ambivalence and manipulation. Employees both embrace and distance themselves from the beliefs and feelings prescribed by the organisation. Working for the company and talking 'Tech culture' are often described as playing a game or participating in a drama. Kunda (1992:161) suggests that this facilitates 'role distancing,' allowing the person to maintain some distance between their company persona and non-company identities. The 'culture' or, to use the Foucauldian terminology, discourses of power, shape and mould the self in potent ways. However, this is not a simple deterministic relationship. The self is constructed in a dialectic of acceptance, resistance and manipulation. This is most explicit in Kunda's analysis of the tension between role embracement and role distancing. In the construction of the organisational self the person is continually 'controlling an ambiguous balance of role embracement and role distancing by engaging in diplomacy, talking the culture, doing it seriously, remembering that it is a game. In short, it is very serious acting' (Kunda 1992:192).

The previous Chapters explored the way individuals interpreted their experience of job loss in narratives. Both romantic and tragic job loss narratives contained descriptions of idealised and desired work careers. In romantic narratives people conceptualised job loss as a positive step toward attaining such a career. In tragic narratives people conceptualised job loss as a threat to attaining such a career, mourning the loss of what 'might have been' if they had not been retrenched. The specific content of idealized and desired careers varied considerably. However, all the idealized career plans shared the characteristic of promising to provide the person with a clear self-narrative that would be the foundation for sustaining other activities in their life. In short, imagined careers in job loss narratives are similar to the career discourses described by Grey (1994) and 'Tech culture' described by Kunda (1992). The desired careers described in Chapters Four, Five, and Six, can be seen as deriving from more general cultural discourses about the role of working in a person's life. However, these cultural discourses about working were not passively accepted. People, to varying degrees, manipulate and transform them to serve their own interests and ends. The next section provides a detailed analysis of this process.

Job Loss Narratives and the Meaning of Working

One of the most significant events for many young school leavers is their first experience of working for an adult wage: 'Having a job comes to signify, through the wage at least, one's independence as an adult, a means of establishing some control over one's own life as an accepted member of the society' (Wilson and Wyn 1978:5). In other words, the idea that a person should work is a shared cultural expectation or discourse about how a person becomes a full member of society. Wilson and Wyn (1978) describe Australian young people's experience of the transition from school to work as a struggle to find a 'livelihood'. The concept of 'livelihood' points to the importance of earning money from employment, while also indicating the less obvious, but no less important, aspects of friendship, independence, skill use, sense of achievement, and community contribution.

While the interviews reported in this study did not specifically examine the transition from school to work, a number of people described their first job as a significant experience in their work history. Geoff, for example, described his first full-time job assembling chairs as 'building myself'.

Doug: What do you think was the most important thing that contributed to that sense of building yourself?

Geoff: Just the fact that I wasn't dependent upon anyone else. My labour was providing my food and my rent and my tyres for my car and my spending money. My labour was providing for my life for the first time really ... So I felt like I was completely responsible for my own life now, completely totally responsible and that was good.

However, Geoff soon left the chair factory in search of more satisfying employment. After a time of unemployment he found a job in The Green Organisation working as a storeman. He worked there for about two years before finishing. This job loss, that Geoff narrated as a strong romance, was analysed in Chapter Four. However, Geoff also described in some detail his experience of working in The Green Organisation prior to his finishing work. During the time he worked there he was gradually given more responsibility and respect by other workers:

Geoff: And suddenly not only was I economically independent and responsible for my own life, but I had responsibilities in the work place as well ... And it just sort of came to me that you've got a job, you're an adult. And it was as simple as that ... and people would take me seriously and they were interested in what I had to say and I started getting invited to peoples places for tea and stuff like that. And for me it was a really noticeable change. And I even found that it started to influence the way I dressed.

Economic independence was not the only benefit of working. Working in The Green Organisation also provided Geoff with a sense of self-worth and value through the responsibilities and status he gained from his employment. Geoff makes clear the interactional sources of his changed self-conception. Other workers began to take him 'seriously'. Being respected as an equal also resulted in changed patterns of interaction, including dinner invitations. Further, Geoff suggests that he began to internalise the norms associated with being a 'respected' worker. He began to feel less comfortable dressing in 'rags' that had previously been his typical attire and more comfortable in 'casual attire' that did not have holes or was not patched. Clothing was an important symbolic support for Geoff's changing self-conception.

However, Geoff did not simply accept his new found status as a working adult. As outlined in Chapter Four, he became increasingly disillusioned with The Green Organisation, until he left with a view to restarting his career as a musician, narrating this transition as a romance. This transformation in Geoff's self-understanding is significant because it clearly portrays the way in which a more general discourse about working as a source of adult identity and livelihood is manipulated and transformed by Geoff to serve his own interests and ends:

Geoff: And it was about that time that I started looking at my history of my relationship to work and to my conception of it, and I'd been looking for a Geoff shaped job and there isn't one, and I've got to make one ... But my project was to get myself into a position where I could have an average wage playing music that I believed in and enjoyed. Because that was what I was best at. I should be able to make a living doing that. And if I'd been that [dedicated] as an electrician, now I would be rolling in dough. Not that I want to be rolling in dough, but it's legitimate and there is a career structure in that field. Just because there isn't one in this field, well sucked in on me really. Not that I think that a traditional career structure is legitimation of what you do, but it means that you can make a living, it means that you can bloody get everyone else off your back and get on with doing what you want to do.

Geoff clearly identifies the cultural and intersubjective sources of a discourse about working for a livelihood. Geoff has internalised this discourse, but does not simply accept it unquestioningly. He experiments with a number of possible careers, exploring, accepting, and rejecting those that do not fit with his interests and desires. He had trained to be a teacher, dropping out of his final year after practical experiences of teaching. He experimented with becoming a classical musician, a paid political activist, and various labouring jobs including his final job at the Green Organisation before his last decision to try to become a popular musician.

However, Geoff does not simply explore various career possibilities, he also is prepared to manipulate and use the discourse about a career to serve his own ends. Specifically, he describes his desire to be seen as pursuing a career as a popular musician as a strategy to 'get everyone else off your back and get on with doing what you want to do'. Geoff uses the discourse about the importance of having a career as a justification for his continuing struggle to become a popular musician. While he has had some success in the past, his current unemployment is explained as a consequence of the absence of a clear career path in popular music rather than as a consequence of personal failure. He specifically refutes the idea that his problems are his fault. He points to how hard he has worked, and that had he chosen to train in an occupation with a clear career path, such as an electrician, he would have been quite successful by now.

Geoff uses and manipulates the cultural expectation that he should have a career, a livelihood, in order to be an accepted member of society. This is a clear example of the way in which narratives learnt and sustained intersubjectively are used and manipulated and not simply accepted by individuals. Subjects need not be passive reflections of a discourse about work as the source of a livelihood. Geoff has learnt and internalised this discourse, it is constitutive of his sense of self. However, he manipulates and reconstructs the discourse as he struggles to find a form of work that he considers morally acceptable and rewarding.

This understanding of self-determination is not an argument for individuals as solitary, autonomous and free from social influence. Rather, it is a form of self-realisation or self-determination that depends on 'hermeneutic reflexivity' (Krogler 1996:37). Geoff is reflexively aware of discourses about the importance of working and having a career that have shaped his understanding of his place in society. It is because he is aware of these influences that he is able to use and manipulate them.

It is not only people who narrated their job loss as a strong romance that can be seen to be using discourses in this way. In weak romances people manipulated a culturally shared discourse about being 'on holiday' to attempt to make sense of their unemployment. However, this claim was not always successful. That is to say, people attempt to interpret their experiences to present themselves in a positive light, but these claims are not always plausible or sustainable.

Tragic Unemployment and the Meaning of Working

Tragic narratives of job loss also use a publicly shared discourse about the importance of having a 'good' career to explain the frustration and anguish associated with both losing a job and unemployment. Three main responses to tragic unemployment were described: searching for a new job, involvement in recreational and educational pursuits, and finally, resignation to unemployment that was associated with severe depression. Lyn's experience, described in Chapters Five and Six, illustrates the first two of these responses clearly.

Lyn, it may be remembered, had been sacked from a secretarial position with no notice. Both the sacking and her ongoing unemployment frustrated her because she desperately wanted a job. She had applied for numerous jobs, knocked on the doors of a number of businesses, and applied to do any training courses for which she was eligible. However, Lyn lived in an outer Melbourne suburb with a higher than average unemployment rate, and she had only minimal educational qualifications. Lyn was unable to find any alternative discourse with which to interpret her experience and, as a consequence, accepted the inconsistency between her unemployed status and an internalised discourse about the importance of working to be an accepted member of adult society. As argued in Chapter Five, this inconsistency is the main source of the frustration and depression described in tragic job loss narratives.

Lyn: It is rather depressing actually. I just thought 'where am I going', I just thought 'what am I doing with my life?' Like, I think some people I know have got jobs and are working and I just think it's not fair ... And I just felt I really want to get a job and I really want to do something with myself and have a future.

Lyn had accepted and internalised a discourse about work as a source of livelihood. However, unlike Geoff, Lyn was unable to manipulate either the discourse, or her current activities, to resolve her distress. In other words, part of that tragic nature of Lyn's experience is that, despite all her attempts, she is unable to manipulate her circumstances or her story to provide a sense of hope.

While Lyn continued to attempt to find another job, other people had resigned themselves to their unemployment. Chapter Six examined the experience of Vince in detail. One of the main characteristics of Vince's narrative was his resignation and sense of powerlessness. This can also be seen as a culturally shared form of discourse that is used by Vince to make sense of and interpret his experience.

Riemann and Schutze (1991:334) develop on Strauss' concept of a trajectory, arguing that it can be used to denote 'disorderly social processes in general that bring about suffering'. While Riemann and Schutze are attempting to develop a sociological discourse about 'trajectories' their analysis also demonstrates the existence a more diffuse cultural discourse about how people understand suffering. Riemann and Schutze suggest that in contrast to the idea of a career that emphasises intentional action, trajectories are characterised by a sense of losing control over one's life and 'being driven' (Riemann and Schutze 1991:336). The person sees themselves as simply reacting to events over which they have no control and which constantly breach their expectations.

The general characteristics of trajectories that 'bring about suffering' described by Riemann and Schutze are also found in the narratives of severe depression during liminal unemployment exemplified in Vince's account. In other words, there is also a shared cultural discourse about helplessness in the face of suffering that is used by Vince to interpret his experience. However, in contrast to Geoff, it is not clear that Vince is aware that he is 'using' a discourse about helplessness in the face of suffering to interpret his experience. I suspect that if this were suggested to Vince he would understand it as implying a form of self-deception on his part. However, the point here is not that Vince is misrepresenting himself through his 'use' of cultural discourses about suffering. Rather, the point is that his self-interpretation is actively constructed from social and cultural resources.

Job Loss and the Gendered Meaning of Working

Chapter Eight demonstrated that work is not always central to a person's self-understanding. Hughes (1959) made a similar point when he observed that 'occupations vary greatly in the degree to which they become the master determinants of the social identity, self-conception, and the social status of the people in them' (Hughes 1959:453). More generally the centrality of work varies by occupation, age and gender, and country (The Meaning of Working International Research Team 1987:83-87). Further, the research reported in Chapter Eight demonstrated that the centrality of work is also variable temporally. One problem with most studies of variations in work centrality is that they typically assume people's orientations to work are relatively stable. The experience of unemployed people points to the in-process nature of the self-identity as part of a continually constructed and reconstructed self-narrative. The centrality of work varies over time as people shuffle the hierarchy of identities and related activities in their lives. The difference in the meaning of working for men and women provides an excellent illustration of this process.

One identity that often is central to the self, and was not discussed in Chapter Eight, is parental identity. One of the criteria for selecting interviewees was that they considered themselves to be 'unemployed'. This excluded people who had left or lost a job for other reasons, including those who had become full-time parents. However, while some people already had adult children, for others finding a long term partner and having children was an important part of their imagined future. The implications of establishing a family were understood quite differently by women compared to men. Women's understandings will be discussed first.

Some women, who had the option open to them, had considered becoming mothers 'supported' by their employed husbands (Lees 1993 provides an excellent critique of the idea that men 'support' women). However, because all respondents considered themselves 'unemployed' none had actually taken up this option. Mary was a thirty year old midwife who had recently bought a house with her partner and whose job loss was narrated as a moderated tragedy, and discussed in Chapter Five. Her understanding of parenthood is representative of most women's responses in the sample. Mary described how much she enjoyed her work as a midwife and then volunteered that, although she did not want to have children at present, she only wanted to work full-time 'another couple of years':

Doug: You want to work another couple of years?
Mary: Yeah. I think if children come along I would probably be looking at part-time work because I feel that it's really important to keep me going and to be interested ... even if it's only one day a week, or two days a week, you're meeting other people, you're learning about things, you know, there's a lot more ongoing in life. And children are only there for a short amount of time. And so, I think it's really good to stay in the workforce so that when they get up and leave, you can go back into it.

If Mary does have children she is not willing to adopt the role of full-time mother and housekeeper to permanently leave paid employment as her mother's generation had largely done. This generational change in the understanding of the relative importance of motherhood and paid employment reflects the rising participation rate of women in the Australian work force from 36 percent in 1966 to 51 per cent in 1991 (Williams 1992:57). While full-time motherhood is still a role adopted by many Australian women (Connell et al. 1982:99), Wilson and Wyn's (1978:40) observation that motherhood 'does not constitute a satisfactory means of livelihood for young women' also applies to many older women such as Mary.

Mary also suggested that paid employment is important as a source of equality and independence in the face of a tradition that restricts women to the role of a financially 'dependent' mother performing home duties:

Doug: Can I ask you how it's affected you financially?

Mary: Well financially not too bad, but I think I'm sort of used to paying my own way, and the financial dependence, I don't like that. Because I've really struggled hard to be equal in the relationship because I've come from an Irish background where the woman is still the one who stays home and looks after the kids and does that and I've never been that type but I'm not going to be now. But the financial dependence is an area where I might have to be. And I don't like that.

Although Mary does not want to become a full-time mother and house keeper, she cannot resist financial dependence on her spouse enforced as a consequence of her unemployment. The financial independence that work provides is one of its most important consequences. Pixley (1993) has recently made the point that for women and men alike the rights and privileges that working for an income provide are difficult to find outside of paid employment. In this study three women and two men described feeling particularly uncomfortable about their financial dependence on their spouses as a consequence of their unemployment.

Working is not only important because it provides financial independence. Dorothy, a 36 year old single parent whose son was a teenager, made this point clearly. She had also been brought up believing that 'men were supposed to work and the women were supposed to stay at home'. However, this is not how things had turned out for her. She had worked full-time in a factory for most of her life. The poverty enforced by unemployment was oppressive, but working was more than simply an income. I asked her: 'So why is work important to you?' She replied: 'It's because I've got nothing else important in my life ... I guess it gives me a purpose in life'.

The expectations that women should stay at home, look after children and not engage in paid employment are part of a discourse that most women in this study described as oppressive and dissatisfying. This discourse was resisted or transformed by these women to serve their own desires and goals, particularly to accommodate their desire to continue in paid employment. These individual transformations of a discourse about motherhood are influenced by broader social changes in the roles of women and they are part of the source of the ongoing inertia of these changes. The counterpart to these changes in women's roles is the slowly changing attitudes to men's roles in childcare and paid employment.

Men still feel a responsibility to earn a wage to 'support' a dependent wife and children. Being unable to find work represents a serious challenge to expectations about the male's role in the family. Bill, a thirty-eight

year old labourer described in Chapter Four, spent considerable time
trying to respond to the question 'Can you give me ten responses to the
question "Who am I?"'

Bill: But I don't think that our society offers much to people apart from work.
          And there's so much that goes along with it. You grow up, you get a
          job, you get a wife and you have some kids and that's it. So if you don't
          have that job... That's why when you say to somebody, tell me who you
          are, or who am I, if they haven't got a job then they just really, they're
          lost.
Doug: It's hard to answer that question?
Bill: Very hard.

Bill's analysis of the significance of working is a particularly masculine
construction. Similar observations were made by a number of males
Part of the frustration of being unemployed for these men is that
employment is understood as a prerequisite for the development of a
stable relationship and becoming part of a 'family'. Unemployment is
painful for Bill because his self-understanding is shaped by his exclusion
from both work and family life. Bill suggests that working provides a
story about the past and an anticipated future. After adolescence he
expected to find a permanent job, become part of a family and, as a
consequence, have a clear sense of his future committed to a home loan
and raising children. The tragic narratives of unemployment underlined
the significance of imagined future employment. Bill's narrative also
points to a tragic exclusion from family life that he attributed to his
repeated experiences of unemployment. While Bill mourned his inability
to attain the ideals of a good career and a family life (patriarchally
conceived) other men struggled to renegotiate their roles in the light of
changing expectations and understandings of a man's role in the family.
Basil was forty-eight years old when interviewed and had been
unemployed for two months after he was retrenched from his job as a
quantity surveyor. Basil's second wife Ethel was a doctor and had recently
given birth to their first baby. Ethel was several years younger than
Basil and as her 'earning potential' was thought to be greater they were
debating whether Basil should take on most of the childcare to allow
Ethel to continue to pursue her career. Until this decision was made
and despite the fact that he was already significantly involved in childcare
Basil considered himself to be 'unemployed'. In the light of his internalised
expectation that he should work, Basil struggled with the idea of taking
on the role of 'househusband'. He explained his discomfort as a consequence

of the inconsistency of the role with the scripts or gendered roles he had been brought up with:

Basil: I suppose also it was usual that if you got married that the guy was the bread winner. And if the wife was working it was usually part-time ... I can't think of anybody when I was growing up where the mother worked and the husband didn't work. Or alternatively where the mother worked full-time and the husband worked part-time.

The labels that Basil uses in the second part of the above quote to differentiate male and female roles indicate the entrenched nature of gender roles in Basil's thought. He uses 'mother' not 'wife' emphasising the female's relationship to her children, and 'husband,' not 'father' emphasising the male's relationship to his wife, not his children. However, Basil was aware of changes in gender roles since his youth and he had begun to question some of his attitudes in the light of the experiences of some of his friends:

Basil: One thing I have wanted to avoid is rushing out and get a job tomorrow. I don't have to do it, so I don't think I should do it ... Like a friend of mine that doesn't work now, but his wife is also a professional and he worked in the same line of business, but she had her career running really hot and she wanted to keep going and they have young kids, the eldest might have just started school, so he has actually become a house father ... So if I just rushed off and got another job tomorrow I would just be out on the same old trip.

Cultural discourses are not accepted unquestioningly, nor do they determine the individual's self-understanding. Basil recognises the gendered, and sexist, form of his understanding of the meaning of working. In the construction of his self-narrative Basil engages in a dialogue with the various possible understandings of the meaning of working. Through narrating his past Basil makes sense of his commitment to working as a central life activity, but he leaves open the possibility of a changed understanding in which childcare would become more important. He describes imagined intersubjective encounters and recounts the experiences of important friends as he struggles to come to a somewhat coherent understanding of his own experience that can be used as a justification for the choices he must now make about how he will act. This is an excellent illustration of the theory of narrative-identity described in Chapter Three. A narrative-identity is constructed out of a remembered biography, cultural repertoires, and real and imagined intersubjective encounters These, in turn, influence choices about how the person then acts.

Repeated Unemployment and Social Change

The ideal of a male full-time life-long job is part of the Fordist mode of regulation of labour and industry at its height from the 1940s to the 1960s in highly industrialised countries. Since the 1970s the Fordist organisation of work has begun to disintegrate (Offe 1985; Williams 1992; Nash 1995). As a consequence, the meanings of working have been changing. McDonald (1994:37) suggests that the meaning of work is splitting in two directions. First, as described earlier in this Chapter, corporations are attempting to manipulate the very personality of the worker (Ezzy, forthcoming). Second, a peripheral or secondary work force is developing where employment is insecure, and inadequate as a foundation for a person's self identity.

Pahl (1995) has examined the effect of the disappearance of the 'job for life' on a group of successful managers. His main concern is 'to explore how far such apparent worldly successes can be transformed into personal successes in reflexively ordering their individual self-identities' (Pahl 1995:121). He argues that with the decline of the old male-dominated career paths, that demanded a person completely invest themselves in their job, people's understanding of success is changing from one emphasising individual power, control and wealth to one emphasising a 'balance' between work and non-work activities such as 'parenting, caring, education or retraining, being unemployed, taking rests between jobs and so on' (Pahl 1995:194).

However, Pahl appears to romanticise unpaid labour. Williams (1992:4) has criticised Pahl's (1984) earlier work *Divisions of Labour* for implying that 'people can rely economically on unpaid forms of work'. Pahl's hope that a balance between paid and unpaid labour will replace the current commitment to paid employment also does not adequately address the financial implications, particularly for the less well off in society. While 'balance' may be possible for wealthy managers, the consequences of 'flexibilization' are more disturbing for those less well off.

A secure job that is enjoyable, financially rewarding, and provides a career-path of progressive advancement clearly emerges as an ideal to which most, if not all, interviewees aspired. A 'career' is a label for an integrally temporal work narrative-identity that is constructed out of a story about where the person has been, what they are doing now, and what they are likely to do in the future. However, an ideal career is not equally accessible to all people. In this study, access to such 'good' jobs was correlated with educational qualifications. The people with the least educational qualifications were those who had often been unemployed repeatedly over their working life, and were employed in short term contract positions that were badly paid and that provided little in the way of a clear future career path.

Haworth (1986:292) points out that unemployment should be seen as disrupting a style of being. Unemployment disrupts both a way of acting in the world, and a way of self-understanding based on a narrative about oneself told to oneself and others. This self-narrative stretches both into the past and into the future. The disappearance of real opportunities to find a 'job for life' has significant implications for those who retain it as an ideal. The consequences of being unable to find stable employment are clearly illustrated in Bill's account. His work history included four periods of unemployment longer than six months, between various short term periods of unskilled labouring:

Bill: I suppose in a sense all the unemployment in my life has disrupted my life... where I'm 38 when I should have settled into a job, but I'm now at a point where I think of the family and the house and all that sort of stuff and I don't have it. Whereas some of our people who certainly did the right thing and stuck their apprenticeships and that and they got married and now a lot of them have got houses and families and they've got their jobs and they're sort of established for the next thirty years of their life, whereas I'm just sort of starting, just starting, I've got no money in the bank and I've just got to wait for my next cheque all the time to keep me going. So I'm on this level, flat, not ascending, just coasting along.

Although losing a job and being unemployed once can be severely disruptive, repeated or prolonged periods of unemployment lead to a new type of lifestyle. Bill's time frame is focused on the present, specifically on the next social security payment. When he does find work he builds up some savings, but these are soon spent during the next period of unemployment, or when he takes a rare holiday. However, it is not simply Bill's finances that are focused on the present and the near future. He mourns the loss of a sense of being 'established'. Being 'established' with a spouse, home loan, and career that provides a plan of what will happen 'for the next thirty years of their life'. In contrast Bill feels that he is 'just starting'. In his more pessimistic moments Bill anticipates that he will never leave a cycle of employment, unemployment, rented accommodation and short term relationships.

Not all people with histories of unemployment remain single and some do buy their own homes. However, in this study people with histories of unemployment described similar frustrations at the disruption to their life caused by repeated unemployment. Further, home ownership and the establishment of a family can exacerbate this sense of frustration because unemployment, particularly if it is prolonged, makes mortgage repayments more difficult and places additional pressures on family relationships.

Bill's experience demonstrates that the ability to resist and transform existing discourses is not distributed equally. Wealthy managers may be able to successfully manipulate a balance between work and non-work activities to provide a satisfying and coherent sense of self. On the other hand, Bill's lack of resources makes repeated periods of unemployment a painful and disruptive experience that only underlines his inability to find a satisfying and socially acceptable form of livelihood. The structure of a self-narrative is powerfully shaped by the past and ongoing events of lived experiences. In contrast to Bill, Geoff had the resources of a very successful educational career to draw on, and Basil owned his own home and his partner was earning enough to financially support both of them. These resources supported their attempts to transform and renegotiate their self-understandings. In other words, while people can narrate their experiences in a variety of ways, the events of lived experience also powerfully shape the narratives that are constructed.

The effects of repeated experiences of unemployment have barely been examined in existing unemployment research. Some people, particularly those who are well resourced, may be able to successfully and creatively make use of the changing organisation of work after the disintegration of the Fordist model of a 'job for life'. Other people find it much more difficult to respond constructively to their changing life circumstances. That is to say, 'economic, cultural and educational resources are necessary preconditions for possible self-realization ... [they] constrain the imagination of socially situated agents as well as their actual possibilities' (Krogler 1996:39). High levels of unemployment and the 'flexibilization' of the labour force are the clear social structural background to the many tragic work histories similar to Bill's.

Fate and Agency in Unemployment Narratives

Stories of unemployment are not simply determined by the events of lived experience. Rather, a complex interweaving of events, narrative strategies, the influences of other people, biographical resources, and cultural repertoires, shape the interpretation of events. MacLachlan and Reid (1994:8) make a similar point in the context of interpretations of literary texts: '[A] text does not have a single meaning determined by a single context; given the interplay of different framings, contexts and therefore meanings are multiple'. The events of lived experience, like texts, can be framed and interpreted in a variety of ways.

Bruner (1990) takes this point a little further when he argues that it is not simply the interpretation of events, but the events of life themselves that are influenced by the form of the narrative told about them: 'we may properly suspect that the shape of a life as experienced is as much dependent upon the narrative skills of the autobiographer as is the story he or she tells about it. It is probably in this sense that Henry James intended his famous remark that 'adventures happen only to people who know how to tell them' (Bruner 1990:163). To use Ricoeur's (1984) phrase, the text, or narrative, has 'two sides'. Lived experience both precedes a narrative, and the narrative shapes practical action. The low self-worth implied in Vince's narrative is difficult to combat precisely because of the influence of Vince's narrative on his actions. 'For instance, actions that require a self-presentation as competent or confident are difficult to negotiate when behavior is mediated by a working self-concept that features the "unsuccessful professional" possible self as a focal point' (Markus and Nurius 1986:962).

The ability to narrate an experience in a particular way is not simply a reflection of a person's 'narrative skills'. Rather, the form of a narrative is also influenced by the events of lived experience. Severe financial distress, for example, makes it extremely difficult to sustain a narrative of job loss as an opportunity for a self-improvement. Further, a narrative is formed in dialogues with close friends and derived from cultural repertoires. Narrative-identities are not creations of isolated individuals. They require intersubjective support in order to be plausible and sustainable.

The complexity of this process is evident in Vince's account. Vince's financial distress whilst unemployed was in part a product of earlier decisions he and his partner had made to purchase a car and to marry. The eight thousand dollar loan they had taken out in order to purchase the car was a considerable financial burden. Further, due to his marital status Vince was no longer eligible for financial assistance from the government when he became unemployed. The decisions to marry and buy a car represent culturally prescribed choices associated with 'normality'. In other words, cultural repertoires shaped Vince's past actions when he was employed, and those actions in turn shaped the experience of unemployment and this, in turn, shaped the form of the narrative he used to interpret his unemployment.

In one sense Vince accurately understands his problem. He is not free to live his life, and tell autobiographical accounts about it, in any way he chooses. Social forces, beyond his control, limit and constrain the events of his life and his interpretation of them. Put another way, the extent to which a person is able to exercise choice, or 'agency', is in part a product of social location. The enduring nature of Vince's past self-narratives, the influence of cultural repertoires, and the constraints imposed by previous decisions all shape his experience and the form of his narrative of that experience. The increasing proportion of jobs that are short-term contracts and the consumerist culture of modern society are two instances of more general social processes that shape both the events of Vince's life, and the narrative that he uses to interpret and respond to these events. However, some of the events of Vince's life, and some aspects of his story could be changed through his own choice and agency. He could, for example, sell his car, or attend a training course. Vince's narrative suppresses and elides his ability to chose and shape his own life. The tragic narrative explains his current troubles in the context of a self portrayal as a helpless victim. The absence of agency in Vince's narrative reduces, in parallel, the possibility of his exercising agency in his own life. However, this sociological analysis of Vince's tragic narrative as an active rhetorical strategy must be seen alongside the equally sociological point that social forces beyond Vince's control have, to a considerable extent, created the difficult circumstance in which Vince finds himself. His inability to exercise choice, to tell a new story that will lead to new actions, is the result of both a rhetorical strategy and the socially structured realities of the events of lived experience.

Self-narratives are not empty rhetoric, pieces of a dream with no foundation in experience. However, rhetoric and subjectivity are integral to the construction of life stories. When I questioned Vince to see if he had any positive visions of the future he described an idea of working as a fishing guide, and then then said: 'Anyway, that's another dream'. While I suspect that Vince is correct, it is possible that Vince may work on his desire to become a fishing guide, resulting in its realization. Indeed, some other interviewees suggested that my questions about their future had led them to think about new possibilities that they had not thought of before. This is an expected outcome of the interview process following on from the recognition of the integral and reciprocal relationship between living a life and telling a life story, and the intersubjective nature of identity.

Individuals sometimes portray themselves as autonomous agents in control of their lives, or on the other hand, victims helpless in the face of their fate and social forces beyond their control. The extent to which people blame or credit themselves for their current situation is in part an expression of the narrative structure of their account. Heroic narratives tend to emphasize agency, tragic stories tend to emphasize the influence of external forces.

Some individuals strategically select between narrative forms depending on the aims and context of their current interlocutors. People such as Geoff and Charles have considerable social, financial, and cultural resources upon which they can draw to enhance both their real opportunities, and their skills as story tellers. On the other hand people such as Vince and Lyn have much more restricted acess to resources of this type. This makes the prospect of successful autonomous action more problematic, with a concomitant tendency to narrate their life as a tragedy, their apparent failure destined by forces beyond their control. More significantly, though it is beyond the scope of this paper, other people have the ability to change some aspects of the social forces that so profoundly shape the experience of the unemployed. This was, of course, Mills' (1970) point when he argued for the differentiation of personal troubles and public issues. The question of how to distinguish empirically between the two is the pivotal problem raised by the preceding analysis of Vince's experience.

9 Conclusion

Summary

This study set out to examine three main issues: the variations in the consequences of job loss, the social construction of the self-concept, and the meaning of working. The experience of job loss provides the substantive focus for the more general questions about self-understanding and the meaning of working. The answers to these three questions are integrally related. Specifically, the variations in the consequences of job loss are explained as a product of the different self-narratives that people use to give both work and job loss meaning.

Chapter Two identified two central problems with existing studies of unemployment: both the temporal aspects of unemployment and the 'subjective' interpretation of 'objective' events are inadequately theorized. The theory developed in the study provides a resolution to these problems. Specifically, the 'objective' events associated with job loss take on meaning as they are interpreted in a 'subjective' narrative that provides a temporal sense of coherence to the self. The variations in the consequences of job loss are explained as a product of the different narratives or stories that people use to interpret their experience. While existing theories of unemployment have provided some important insights, the theory of job loss developed in this study deals more incisively with the complexities of the experience.

The theory of narrative-identity developed in the study captures the complexity, subtlety and dynamism of the processual construction of the self-concept. Narrative-identities and more specifically narratives about job loss, are not solely determined by the events of lived experience. People are able to tell a variety of stories about their experience. Some people use this flexibility to strategically further their own interests. On the other hand, narrative-identities are not free fictions. The events of lived experience frame the narrative, limiting and enabling various forms of interpretation. This dynamic interplay between the events of lived experience and their interpretation in narrative is at the heart of the variations in the response to job loss. For example, the sudden termination of employment and repeated rejections of job applications may be framed by a tragic narrative emphasising the importance of the job that was lost and the difficulty of finding new employment. This may lead people into passive acceptance of unemployment and a sense of despair. Alternatively, sudden termination of employment may be celebrated as an opportunity to embark on a new career. The job loss may be framed by a romantic narrative and supported by promising new opportunities that encourage a person to be hopeful about their future in a new career. The consequences of the job loss are not determined solely by the 'objective' events of the passage, or solely by the 'subjective' response people construct. The consequences of a job loss are a product of the dynamic interplay between events and their interpretation that is captured precisely by a narrative conception of identity.

The dynamic interplay between the events of lived experience and their interpretation in narrative is also integral to the temporal variations in people's response to job loss and unemployment. New opportunities and changed circumstances may give a person new hope in their search for employment. However, new opportunities can, in some ways, be created as a consequence of a more hopeful narrative about the experience of unemployment. For example, Chapter Four describes Bill's decision to become more active whilst unemployed. Bill's changed understanding led to new types of activity that in turn increased his job prospects. Similarly, in ironic tragedies interviewees describe a change in interpretation (Chapter Five). Job loss was initially celebrated as a release from an oppressive occupation, but as the period of unemployment lengthened, and the rejection of job applications accumulated, their attitude toward the last job changed to the extent that, at the time of the interview, the decision to leave the last job was seen as a mistake. These temporal transformations in people's understanding of job loss underline the dynamic interplay between the events of lived experience and their narrative interpretation.

Chapter Eight discussed the meaning of working, making the point that cultural discourses and individual narratives are also mutually influential. Cultural discourses about the importance of having a career are internalised and influence most people's narratives about the place of paid employment in their own lives. However, these cultural discourses do not determine the shape or content of an individual's narrative-identity. Rather, they are used as resources. Individuals variously accept, reject, manipulate and transform cultural discourses about the meaning of working. The ongoing struggle to find 'good work' variously transforms, modifies and maintains these cultural discourses.

Working is primarily important because it sustains a narrative-identity that provides a sense of personal continuity through time. This sense of personal coherence is grounded in and derives from regular activities, cultural discourses, and intersubjective encounters (both real and imagined). Job loss may disrupt some or all of these supports of a person's narrative-identity. However, because self-narratives are always 'in process' the job loss passage may be narrated in a variety, though not unlimited, number of ways. Whether a tragedy or a romance, the form of the soliloquy that forms a person's self-narrative is shaped by their anticipated future. Tragedies typically describe a biographical trajectory out of a valued past into a devalued and unpleasant future. Romances, in contrast, anticipate a future of gradually improving rewards and opportunities. The remembered past and imagined futures are interwoven with the events of the present, using available cultural resources to construct a narrative-identity that gives present experiences meaning and provides a basis for choosing how to act. A narrative conception of identity captures the complexity and subtlety of this process that is the basis of the variations in responses to job loss.

Future Directions

There are a number of ways in which the research could have been extended and improved. Longitudinal data would have provided a much richer source of information about temporal changes to individual's narrative-identities. Ideally, respondents would have been interviewed both before and after their job loss. However, obtaining permission to interview people who are about to be retrenched is typically only possible if people have a long notice period. Similarly, repeated interviews over the first year of unemployment would provide a clearer picture of the process of change in individuals' narratives (Wiersma 1992).

Since Bakke's (1934) examination of unemployment in the nineteen thirties a number of qualitative studies have observed that reduced income has significant effects on people's relationships (Burman 1988; Turner 1983; Marsden and Duff 1975; Carr-Hill 1984; Sinfield 1981). Quantitative studies have also demonstrated that financial strain is strongly correlated with indicators of mental health (Rowley and Feather 1987; Gurney 1980; Warr 1984; Kessler et al. 1988). The present study has underlined the significance of financial remuneration as a part of the job loss passage. Financial security moderates the trauma of job loss and helps sustain a narrative of hope about the future. However, the influence of money on both narrative-identities and social relationships deserves further research.

Sociology lacks a 'serious discussion of money' (Smelt 1980:204). While there has been some important recent work by Zelizer (1994) on the various meanings of money and Ritzer (1995) on credit cards, Simmel (1990) remains one of the most perceptive analysts of the subjective significance of money. Simmel argued that money is a particular generalised form of possession. According to Simmel the significance of possessions is intrinsically temporal: 'Static possession exists only in the imaginary aftermath of the processes that precede it, and in the imaginary anticipation of future enjoyment or use. If one disregards these processes which one falsely considers to be only secondary, then nothing remains of the concept of property' (Simmel 1990:306). The possession of money provides a more generalised anticipation of the future enjoyment of possessions: 'Possession of money implies the possibility of enjoyment of an indefinite number of objects' (Simmel 1990:309). In other words, Simmel emphasises the significance of the imagined future use of money. This is consistent with the observed significance of imagined futures in all forms of job loss narratives. The possession of money or the assurance that a person will be paid sustains the plausibility of their imagined future.

It is not possible to narrate one's experience in any way one chooses. The events of lived experience are an obdurate 'reality' that shape and significantly influence the narrative that can be plausibly told. One of the most significant concrete consequences of working is remuneration. Money facilitates many of the activities that people undertake in their lives. Money also facilitates relationships. In an increasingly consumer oriented modern society, without adequate finances it is often difficult to participate in the activities through which friendships are developed and sustained. These aspects of money also deserve more explicit attention.

Cultural discourses are politically contested (Somers and Gibson 1994:73). One of the tasks of the researcher is therefore to analyse contradictions and consistencies between specific narratives and cultural discourses or sedimented traditions (Passerini 1989:194; Freeman 1984:15). The previous Chapters pointed in various ways to the tension between the ideal of a life-long career and the rapidly diminishing availability of concrete job opportunities through which this ideal can be attained. The 'flexibilization' of the labour force, including short term contracts and part-time work, has significantly reduced the number of permanent jobs available. This has a number of profound implications for the meaning of working in contemporary society. Beck (1992), for example, has pointed to the inconsistencies between a society organised around full-time life-long wage labour and the flexibilization of the labour force through the rapid growth of part-time and casual work:

> Industrial society is a wage labor society through and through in the plan of
> its life, in its joys and sorrows, in its concept of achievement, in its justification
> of inequality, in its social welfare laws, in its balance of power and in its

politics and culture. If it is facing a systematic transformation of wage labor then it is facing a social transformation. (Beck 1992:140)

It is possible that higher levels of unemployment, underemployment, and job insecurity are not a transitional effect, but an indicator of a change in the basic structure of the employment system. In this scenario unemployment and job insecurity will become a regular part of the lived experience of a growing portion of the population (Beck 1992:149). If this is the case, studies of unemployment should examine the changing nature of the self-narratives of people in these short-term and part-time occupations. At issue here is how the increasingly insecure nature of work in modern society is shaping people's life-plans, narrative-identities, and day to day coping strategies.

These issues are also clearly linked to other forms of job loss involving, for example, transitions into full-time childcare, or part-time work and part-time childcare. The gender differences in these experiences is also an issue that deserves further and careful research. More generally, the research could be extended by using a wider sampling strategy to examine a broader ranger of transitions in and out of employment.

Conclusion

John Lennon said: 'Work is life, you know, and without it, there's nothing but fear and insecurity' (quoted in Solt and Egan 1988:75). Paid work is only one form of work in humanity's short history. Nonetheless employment dominates contemporary life in many ways, perhaps most graphically illustrated by the dominance of modern cities' skylines by skyscrapers, the cathedrals of big business. On the other hand, most contemporary experiences of unemployment are characterised by people's inability to find meaning outside of paid employment. However, this way of framing the problem emphasises the actions of the individual and does not adequately address how these are constrained by the organisation of society. Alternatively it could be said that modern society is increasingly condemning people to lives in which they are unable to construct a sense of purpose either because they cannot find employment, or the employment they can find is degrading.

This study has explored some of the ways in which people construct, or fail to construct, a worthwhile life after losing a job. Integral to romantic job loss narratives, and a sense of hope during unemployment, is an imagined future that is satisfying and rewarding. Most existing studies of unemployment and of the meaning of work make no attempt to explore the role of an imagined future. Nor do they examine how individuals adapt and manipulate experiences in the present to provide themselves with a sense of hope for the future. In short, most existing studies are framed as tragedies, leaving a sense of inevitability about the problems of unemployment or the oppressive nature of work. This represents a failure both at the analytic level, to unmask the social processes of reality construction and power relations, and a failure at the policy level, to ask how things could be otherwise.

This study has focused on how individuals cope with and respond to job loss. However, if unemployment and underemployment are becoming an increasingly common experience in modern societies one of the most important issues that needs now to be explored is how changes in social structure (the macro equivalent of lived experience) and culture (the macro equivalent of narrative-identities) can provide a sense of hope for the future.

Appendix: Thinking about Methodology

Previous studies of unemployment fall into two basic genres. On the one hand are quantitative, statistically representative studies using forced response measures of psychological well-being. On the other hand are qualitative studies, rich in descriptive detail, but lacking any attempt to develop the theoretical implications of their observations. The present study is significantly different to both these approaches. A theoretically sophisticated analysis of long interviews with a small group of respondents allows the processes associated with unemployment to be described in detail. The aim of the research is not to identify what proportion of people use tragic or romantic narratives. Rather, the aim is to show what social psychological processes are involved in the production of tragic and romantic narratives.

A qualitative study that focuses on social psychological processes provides a much more sophisticated understanding of what happens to unemployed people. In particular, the methodology provides a complex analysis of the different interpretations and meanings unemployed people give to their experience. A number of unemployment researchers have recently called for qualitative studies for similar reasons. Pernice (1996) for example, calls for qualitative studies of unemployment to provide an understanding of the complexities of unemployment that is sophisticated enough to formulate effective solutions.

Reality, Interpretation, and Autobiography

I distinguish between the 'objective' events of lived experience, and the 'subjective' interpretation of these events in a narrative. The interactionist tradition typically does not attempt to differentiate lived experience from its configuration in narrative. Interactionist studies typically maintain a realistic orientation to the stories of their interviewees. The information gained in interviews is taken to simply and accurately reflect lived experience (Denzin 1992:119). On the other hand, some studies, influenced by postmodernism and cultural studies, make a radical distinction between narrative and lived experience. Linde for example, argues that the actual facts of a person's life are irrelevant to her study: 'all we can ever work with is texts of one sort or another' (Linde 1993:14). While

Linde is partially correct in the sense that all action is textually mediated, she tends toward the closed semanticism that fails to deal with exigencies of practical action. The skeptical postmodernist analyses of the role of language, of which Linde's work is an example, set up a false dichotomy. Either language is transparent and reflects lived experience accurately, or it is a distorting screen that always projects experience out of its own categories.

If language is viewed as unavoidably distorting understanding and there is no criteria that can be used to judge an explanation's correctness, then all explanations of events are 'equally legitimate and adequate' (Spence 1988:68). This understanding typically rests on an argument for the underlying disorder of 'reality'. 'Reality' is conceived to be indescribable and there is a radical disjunction between reality and narrative. Following Ricoeur, I argue that this dichotomy is a false one. It demonstrates a misunderstanding of the hermeneutic point about the nature of reality and can be seen as the result of a lingering positivism that attempts to deny the linguistically mediated nature of the events of lived experience (Bruner 1990:111). Rather, in Ricoeur's (1991a) provocative phrase, life is 'in quest of a narrative'. It is erroneous to assume that life is lived and not told. Action is understood in the same way as the plot of a narrative. Action is always symbolically mediated, symbols acting as a quasi-text that allow conduct to be interpreted. The events of lived experience have a pre-narrative quality, they are a nascent story. Life is 'an activity and a passion in search of a narrative' (Ricoeur 1991a:29).

Following Merleau-Ponty, Polkinghorne (1988:26) suggests that language brings the real to human experience: 'Languages may be the device that allows reality to show forth in experience. Rather than standing in the way of the experience of the real, language may be the lens whose flexibility makes reality appear in sharp focus before experience'. Meaning, Ricoeur argues, is not merely the result of a projection of our understandings onto a meaningless series of events. Rather, the events of lived experience have an 'inchoate narrativity that does not proceed from projecting ... literature on life, but that constitute a genuine demand for narrativity' (Ricoeur 1984:74).

Both the events of lived experience and imaginative configuration are represented in narratives. The task of theory is to explain the relationship between the two. This point is well illustrated in Langer's (1991) analysis of holocaust testimonies. Rather than attempting to describe what 'really' happened in the holocaust, or simply discussing the text of the narratives, Langer focuses on the process of construction of the narrative, and the method of communication to expose the destructive nature of survivor's experiences. The form of the narrative is representative of the form of the experience, and it is through examining the process by which this is achieved that a greater understanding is gained.

Language, or more specifically dialogue, also plays a central role in constructing self-identity. The self discovered in interviews is not an unchanging substance or 'real' life history. Rather, interviews are sites where autobiography is actively constructed. Bruner observes that whilst conducting autobiographical interviews, 'very soon we discovered that we were listening to people *in the act of constructing* a longitudinal version of self (Bruner 1990:120, emphasis added). However, it is not simply the past that is being actively constructed. Jackson (1994:823) notes that her interviewees were 'not just reflecting on experience, but using the opportunity provided by the interview situation to actively configure future experience'. The narration of a life history as it is configured around a central plot represents both the influence of the biographical past, hopes for the future, and the current situation of the interviewee. In other words, this understanding of interview narratives is consistent with Ricoeur's three moments of narrative emplotment: past, present and future.

Positivist methodologies try to prevent or avoid the influence of subjective understandings in interviews. However, subjective interpretations are precisely the focus of narrative analysis (Ezzy 1998b). From this perspective the important issue is not that narrators represent their lives accurately in interviews. Rather, 'it is enough to note that they believe they are doing so. This belief is at the base of their struggles to tell their stories correctly...' (Rosenwald 1992:271). That is to say, the focus of the research is the way people tell their stories and the relationship between experience and narrative, rather than the accuracy or otherwise of the account.

Theoretical Sampling

As defined by Corbin and Strauss (1990:9) 'theoretical sampling' involves a process where the 'representativeness of concepts, not of persons is crucial'. The aim is not simply to generalise the findings to the broader population, but to construct a theoretical explanation by specifying the conditions and process that give rise to the variations in a phenomenon. Thus the units of analysis are concepts, and the representativeness is of the theoretical complexity of the phenomena being described.

Strauss (1970) succinctly summarises that strategy of theoretical sampling:

> In theoretical sampling, the basic question is: What groups or subgroups does one turn to next in data collection? And for what theoretical purpose? Since possibilities of choice are infinite, choice is made according to theoretical criteria ... The directed collection of data through theoretical sample leads eventually to a sense of closure. Core and subsidiary categories emerge. Through data collection there is a 'saturation' of those categories. Hypotheses at varying levels of abstraction are developed (they embrace the categories). Those hypotheses are validated or qualified through directed collection of data. (Strauss 1970:52)

The sample size was determined on theoretical as opposed to statistical grounds. Specifically, Strauss and Corbin suggest that the important criterion for the ending of field work is 'theoretical saturation'. They define theoretical saturation as occurring when:

> (1) no new or relevant data seem to emerge regarding a category; (2) the category development is dense, insofar as all of the paradigm elements are accounted for, along with variation and process; (3) the relationships between categories are well established and validated. (Strauss and Corbin 1990:188)

In the case of the current research, there were still a number of categories and experiences that could have been fruitfully explored and that were not 'saturated'. There is always more that can be explored. However, the central categories of the analysis were theoretically saturated.

The Sample

Thirty-three people in total were interviewed, comprising fourteen women and nineteen men. Their average age was 37 years old, withn a range of 22 to 60 years. Their occupations also represent a broad range, varying from a badly paid casual cleaner to a highly paid corporate manager. Most of the participants were interviewed between August 1993 and July 1994 with a few additional interviews conducted during late 1994. Five of these participants had two job losses within the last year. Therefore, from the 33 interviews 38 job loss narratives were obtained. Participants were obtained through contact with a company that had announced intended staffing reductions, through a group of community organisations for the unemployed known as 'SkillShares', and through snowballing from these respondents.

The focus of the current research on job loss as a passage, as opposed to unemployment as a status, circumvents to some extent the highly problematic question of deciding who is to be included in the category of 'unemployed'. The following criteria were used to define potential respondents: people who had lost or left a full-time job no more than one year ago and who had subsequently been without employment for at least one month and described themselves as unemployed. These restrictions were designed to identify people who had some experience of being unemployed, and whose memories of the job loss event were reasonably recent. In order to facilitate detailed analysis of central categories several types of workers were excluded from consideration. These included part-time workers, recent immigrants, retirees, and people leaving work to take up full-time childcare. These categories of workers were excluded on the grounds that the complexities associated with their experiences were beyond the scope of the study. These experiences deserve more careful study in their own right. For example, non-English speakers' experience of job loss is also complicated by their experiences of racism and ethnocentrism in a society that generally assumes they are able to speak English.

Data Analysis

Thematic analysis was employed to identify the structures or form of the job loss experience (Miles and Huberman 1994:245-262; Kellehear 1993:38-42; Van Manen 1990:79). Thematic analysis, as developed in grounded theory (Glaser and Strauss 1967), inductively identifies concepts and categories in the data. The identification of themes occurred at two levels. First, I focused on the events of lived experience. Here I attempted to identify themes across the whole set of respondents, searching for similar and contrasting events. These were then coded and compared to identify the main properties of the passages (Glaser and Strauss 1971). A 'property' is a variable or conceptual dimension. For example, a passage may be more or less planned or there may have been ample or very little notice. I also searched for relationships between various properties of the status passages, being particularly concerned to identify the relationship between properties and self-evaluations.

Second, I analysed the shape or form of the narrative of the job loss as a whole (Riessman 1993; Cortazzi 1993). There are a wide variety of definitions of what constitutes a narrative and an equally wide variety of approaches to the analysis of these narratives (Robinson and Hawpe 1986:112; Riessman 1993:17-18). The analysis of narrative form reported here followed that employed by Gergen and Gergen (Gergen and Gergen 1988; Gergen 1988; 1992; 1994). The advantage of their methodology is that it examines the relationship between narrative plot and self-evaluations, and this is the focus on the current research. Other forms of narrative analysis are less concerned with the evaluative dimensions of the narrative (Riessman 1993; Cortazzi 1993).

Ethical Issues

In order to protect interviewees confidentiality, all names have been changed. Approval for the research was gained from the appropriate University ethics committee. Letters of approval were also obtained from the management of the two organisations involved in the research. None of the interviewees indicated feeling threatened or compromised by the interview process. One of the ambiguities I experienced whilst conducting long intensive interviews was that the mutual trust developed during the interview had no place in an ongoing relationship. Interviewees often revealed quite personal feelings about their experiences and some cried as they discussed particularly painful events in their past. My feelings of incongruence were sometimes exacerbated by the isolation and distress that some people described as their experience of unemployment. Similarly, at the end of the interview, I left with 'the data' and the interviewee was left with the memory of a conversation.

However, several people explicitly commented that they found the interview useful and worthwhile because it helped them to understand and come to terms with their experience. For example, after I asked Judy what her plans were she spent some time attempting to describe her hopes and thoughts about the various possibilities. Then she said:

Judy: That is helpful. I didn't know that until now.
Doug: What do you mean?
Judy: Well, I guess in terms of realising that I am thinking quite a bit about what direction should I go.

Judy's comments are consistent with the earlier observation that interviews involve the construction of biographies as much as they involve the description of pre-existing biographical narratives.

Bibliography

Anderson, H. and Goolishian, H. (1992) 'The Client is the Expert', in S. McNamee and K. Gergen (eds), *Therapy as Social Construction*, London: Sage.

Archer, J. and Rhodes, V. (1987) 'Bereavement and reactions to job loss: A comparative review', *British Journal of Social Psychology*, 26: 211-224.

Atchley, R. (1976) *The Sociology of Retirement*, New York: John Wiley & Sons.

Athens, L. (1994) 'The Self as a Soliloquy', *The Sociological Quarterly*, 35: 521-532.

Bakke, E. (1934) *The Unemployed Man*, New York: E. P. Dutton and Co.

Ball, D. (1976) 'Failure in Sport', *American Sociological Review*, 41: 726-239.

Beck, U. (1992) *Risk Society*, trans. M. Ritter, London: Sage.

Berger, P. (1966) *Invitation to Sociology*, Harmondsworth: Penguin.

Blumer, H. (1969) *Symbolic Interactionism*, New Jersey: Prentice Hall.

Braverman, H. (1974) *Labour and Monopoly Capital*, New York: Monthly Review Press.

Breakwell, G. (1984) 'Young people in and out of work', in B. Roberts, R. Finnegan and D. Gallie (eds), *New Approaches to Economic Life*, Manchester: Manchester University Press.

Brown, A. (1990) *The Social Processes of Aging and Old Age*, Engelwood Cliffs: Prentice Hall.

Bruner, J. (1986) *Actual Minds, Possible Worlds*, Cambridge Mass.: Harvard University Press.

Bruner, J. (1987) 'Life as Narrative', *Social Research*, 54, 1: 11-32.

Bruner, J. (1990) *Acts of Meaning*, Harvard: Harvard University Press.

Burman, P. (1988) *Killing Time, Losing Ground; Experiences of Unemployment*, Toronto: Wall and Thompson.

Carr, D. (1985) 'Life and the Narrator's Art', in H. Silverman and D. Ihde (eds), *Hermeneutics and Deconstruction*, New York: State University of New York Press.

Carr-Hill, R. (1984) 'Whither (research on) unemployment?', in B. Roberts, R. Finnegan and D. Gallie (eds), *New Approaches to Economic Life*, Manchester: Manchester University Press.

Charmaz, K. (1991) *Good Days, Bad Days: The Self in Chronic Illness and Time*, New Jersey: Rutgers University Press.

Charmaz, K. (1994) 'Identity Dilemmas of Chronically Ill Men', *The Sociological Quarterly*, 35: 269-288.

Connell, R., Ashenden, D., Kessler, S. and Dowsett, G. (1982) *Making the Difference*, Sydney, George Allen and Unwin.

Cooley, C. (1956) *Human Nature and the Social Order*, Gencoe, Ill.: The Free Press.

Cortazzi, M. (1993) *Narrative Analysis*, London: The Falmer Press.

Cronon, W. (1992) 'A Place for Stories: Nature, History and Narrative', *Journal of American History*, 78: 1347-1376.

Cutler, T. (1978) 'The Romance of "Labour" ', *Economy and Society*, 7:75-95.

de Certeau, M. (1984) *The Practice of Everyday Life*, trans. S. Rendall, Berkeley: University of California Press.

Denzin, N. (1989) *Interpretive Interactionism*, Newbury Park: Sage.

Denzin, N. (1992) *Symbolic Interactionism and Cultural Studies*, Cambridge Mass.: Blackwell.

Dunne, J. (1995) 'Beyond sovereignty and deconstruction: the storied self', *Philosophy and Social Criticism*, 21: 137-157.

Eisenberg, P. and Lazarsfeld, P. (1938) 'The Psychological Effects of Unemployment', *The Psychology Bulletin*, 35: 358-372.

Elder, G. (1985) 'Perspectives on the Life Course', in G. Elder (ed.), *Life Course Dynamics*, Ithaca: Cornell University Press.

Epston, D. and White, M. (1992) *Experience, Contradiction, Narrative and Imagination*, South Australia: Dulwich Centre Publications.

Ezzy, D. (1993) 'Unemployment and Mental Health: A Critical Review', *Social Science and Medicine*, 37: 41-52.

Ezzy, D. (1997) 'Subjectivity and the Labour Process: Conceptualising "Good Work"', *Sociology*, 31: 427-444.

Ezzy, D. (1998a) 'Theorizing Narrative-Identity: Symbolic Interactionism and Hermeneutics', *The Sociological Quarterly*, 39: 239-252.

Ezzy, D. (1998b) 'Lived Experience and Interpretation in Narrative Theory: Experiences of Living with HIV/AIDS', *Qualitative Sociology*, 21: 169-180.

Ezzy, D. (2000) 'Fate and Agency in Job Loss Narratives', *Qualitative Sociology*, 23: 121-134.

Ezzy, D. (forthcoming) 'A simulacrum of workplace community: Individualism and engineered culture', *Sociology: The Journal of the British Sociological Association*.

Feather, N. (1990) *The Psychological Impact of Unemployment*, New York: Springer-Verlag.

Feather, N. (1992) 'Expectancy-value theory and unemployment effects', *Journal of Occupational and Organizational Psychology*, 65: 315-330.

Feather, N. (1997) 'Economic Deprivation and the psychological Impact of Unemployment', *The Australian Psychologist*, 32, 1: 37-45.

Feather, N. and Davenport, R. (1981) 'Unemployment and Depressive Affect: A Motivational and Attributional Analysis', *Journal of Personality and Social Psychology*, 41, 3: 422-436.

Feather, N. and O'Brien, G. (1986) 'A longitudinal analysis of the effects of different patterns of employment and unemployment on school leavers', *British Journal of Psychology*, 77: 459-479.

Fineman, S. (1983) *White Collar Unemployment, Impact and Stress*, New York: John Wiley.

Ford, H. (1923) *My Life and Work*, Sydney: Angus and Robertson.

Freeman, M. (1984) 'History, Narrative, and Life-Span Developmental Knowledge', *Human Development*, 27: 1-19.

Frye, N. (1957) *Anatomy of Criticism*, New Jersey: Princeton University Press.

Fryer, D. (1985) 'Stages in the psychological response to unemployment: A (dis)integrative review', *Current Psychological Research Review*, 4: 257-273.

Fryer, D. (1986) 'Employment deprivation and personal agency during unemployment: A critical discussion of Jahoda's explanation of the psychological effects of unemployment', *Social Behaviour*, 1: 3-23.

Fryer, D. (1992) 'Psychological or Material Deprivation', in E. McLauglin (ed.), *Understanding Unemployment*, London: Routledge.

Fryer, D. (1995) 'Agency Theory', in N. Nicholson (ed.), *Dictionary of Organizational Behaviour*, Oxford: Blackwell.

Fryer, D. and Payne, R. (1984) 'Proactive Behaviour in Unemployment: Findings and Implications', *Leisure Studies*, 3: 273-295.

Fryer, D. and Payne, R. (1986) 'Being Unemployed: A Review of the Literature on the Psychological Experience of Unemployment', *International Review of Industrial and Organization Psychology*, C. Cooper and I. Robertson (eds), Chichester: Wiley.

Fryer, D. and Winefield, H. (1998) 'Employment stress and unemployment distress as two varieties of labour market induced psychological strain', *The Australian Journal of Social Research*, 5: 3-18.

Garfinkel, H. (1967) *Studies in Ethnomethodology*, Engelwood Cliffs, New Jersey: Prentice-Hall.

Gergen, K. and Gergen, M. (1988) 'Narrative and the Self as Relationship', *Advances in Experimental Psychology*, 21: 17-56.

Gergen, K. and Kaye, J. (1993) 'Beyond Narrative in the Negotiation of Therapeutic Meaning', in K. Gergen (ed.), *Refiguring Self and Psychology*, Dartmouth: Aldershot.

Gergen, M. (1988) 'Narrative structures in social explanation', in C. Antaki (ed.), *Analysing Everyday Explanation*, London: Sage.

Gergen, M. (1992) 'Life Stories: Pieces of a Dream', in G. Rosenwald and R. Ochberg (eds), *Storied Lives: The Cultural Politics of Self-Understanding*, New Haven and London: Yale University Press.

Gergen, M. (1994) 'The Social Construction of Personal Histories', in T. Sarbin and J. Kitsuse (eds), *Constructing the Social*, London: Sage.

Glaser, B. and Strauss, A. (1967) *The Discovery of Grounded Theory*, Chicago: Aldine.

Glaser, B. and Strauss, A. (1971) *Status Passage*, London: Routledge and Kegan Paul.

Goffman, E. (1963) *Stigma*, Harmondsworth: Penguin.

Goffman, E. (1967) *Interaction Ritual,* Harmondsworth: Penguin.

Goffman, E. (1976) *Asylums,* Harmondsworth: Penguin.

Goldthorpe, J., Lockwood, D., Bechhofer, F. and Platt, J. (1968) *The Affluent Worker: Industrial Attitudes and Behaviour*, Cambridge: Cambridge University Press.

Graetz, B. (1990) 'Health Consequences of Employment and Unemployment', Paper presented at The Australian Longitudinal Survey: Social and Economic Policy Research Conference.

Grey, C. (1994) 'Career as a project of the self and labour process discipline', *Sociology*, 28: 479-497.

Hakim, C. (1983) 'The Social Consequences of High Unemployment', *Journal of Social Policy*, 11, 4: 433-67.

Hammarstrom, A. and Janlert, U. (1997) 'Nervous symptoms in a longitudinal study of youth unemployment - selection or exposure', *Journal of Adolescence*, 20: 293-305.

Harris, D. (1978) 'The Consequences of Failure in Sport', *Urban Life*, 7: 177-188.

Hartley, J. (1980) 'The impact of unemployment upon the self-esteem of managers', *Journal of Occupational Psychology*, 53: 147-155.

Hartley, J. and Fryer, D. (1984) 'The Psychology of Unemployment: A Critical Appraisal', in G. Stephenson and J. Davis (eds), *Progress in Applied Social Psychology*, vol. 2, Chichester: Wiley.

Haworth, J. (1986) 'Meaningful activity and psychological models of non-employment', *Leisure Studies*, 5: 281-297.

Hayes, J. and Nutman, P. (1981) *Understanding the Unemployed*, London: Tavistock.

Heidegger, M. (1962) *Being and Time*, trans J. Macquarie and E. Robinson, Oxford: Blackwell.

Hepworth, S. (1980) 'Moderating factors of the psychological impact of unemployment', *Journal of Occupational Psychology*, 53: 139-45.

Hermans, H., Trix, I. and Kempen, H. (1993) 'Internal Dialogues in the Self: Theory and Method', *Journal of Personality*, 61: 207-236.

Hill, J. (1978) 'The psychological impact of unemployment', *New Society*, 43: 118-120.

Hughes, E. (1959) 'The Study of Occupations', in R. Merton, L. Broom, and L. Cottrell (eds), *Sociology Today*, vol. 2, New York: Harper and Row.

Jackson, J. (1994) 'The Rashomon Approach to Dealing with Chronic Pain', *Social Science and Medicine*, 38: 823-833.

Jackson, P., Stafford, E., Banks, M. and Warr, P. (1983) 'Unemployment and Psychological distress in Young People: The Moderating Role of Employment Commitment', *Journal of Applied Psychology*, 68: 525-535.

Jackson, T. (1999) 'Differences in psychosocial experiences of employed, unemployed, and student samples of young adults', *Journal of Psychology*, 133: 49-54.

Jahoda, M. (1980) 'One model of man or many?' In A. Chapman and D. Jones (eds), *Models of Man*, Leicester: British Psychological Society.

Jahoda, M. (1981), 'Work, Employment and Unemployment', *American Psychologist*, 31: 184-191.

Jahoda, M. (1982) *Employment and Unemployment*, Cambridge: Cambridge University Press.

Jahoda, M. (1984) 'Social institutions and human needs: A comment on Fryer and Payne', *Leisure Studies*, 3: 297-299.

Jahoda, M. (1986) 'In Defence of a Non-Reductionist Social Psychology', *Social Behaviour*, 1: 25-29.

Jahoda, M. (1988) 'Economic recession and mental health', *Journal of Social Issues*, 44: 13-23.

Jahoda, M., Lazarsfeld, P. and Zeisel, H. (1971) [1933] *Marienthal: The Sociography of an Unemployed Community*. London: Tavistock.

Kabanoff, B. (1982) 'Psychological effects of unemployment', *Australia and New Zealand Journal of Psychiatry*, 16: 37-42.

Kearl, M. (1987) 'Knowing how to quit: on the finitudes of everyday life', *Sociological Inquiry*, 56: 283-303.

Kellehear, A. (1990) *Dying of Cancer: The Final Year of Life*, New York: Harwood.

Kellehear, A. (1993) *The Unobtrusive Researcher: A guide to methods*, Sydney: Allen and Unwin.

Kelvin, P. (1984) 'The historical dimension of social psychology: the case of unemployment', in H. Tajfel (ed.), *The Social Dimension*, vol. 2, Cambridge: Cambridge University Press.

Kelvin, P. and Jarret, J. (1985) *Unemployment: Its social psychological effects*, Cambridge: Cambridge University Press.

Kemp, P. (1995) 'Ricoeur between Heidegger and Levinas', *Philosophy and Social Criticism*, 21: 41-61.

Kessler, R., Turner, J. and House, J. (1988) 'Effects of Unemployment on Health in a Community Survey: Main, Modifying, and Mediating Effects', *Journal of Social Issues*, 44: 69-85.

Kitson, G., Babri, K., Roach, M. and Placidi, K. (1989) 'Adjustment to Widowhood and Divorce: A Review', *Journal of Family Issues*, 10: 5-32.

Knights, D. (1990) 'Subjectivity, Power and the Labour Process', in D. Knights and H. Willmott (eds), *Labour Process Theory*, London: Macmillan.

Kohen, J. (1981) 'From Wife to Family Head: Transitions in Self-Identity', *Psychiatry*, 44: 230-240.

Kohn, M. and Schooler, C. (1983) *Work and Personality*, New Jersey: Alex Pub. Co.

Komarovsky, M. (1940) *The unemployed man and his family*, New York: Dryden Press (Reprinted by Arno Press, 1971).

Kriegler, R. (1980) *Working for the Company*, Melbourne: Oxford University Press.

Krogler, H. (1996) 'The self-empowered subject', *Philosophy and Social Criticism*, 22: 13-44.

Kubler-Ross, E. (1969) *On Death and Dying*, London: Macmillan.

Kuhn, M. and McPartland, T. (1954), 'An Empirical Investigation of Self-Attitudes', *American Sociological Review*, 19: 68-76.

Kunda, G. (1992) *Engineering Culture*, Philadelphia: Temple University Press.

Langer, L. (1991) *Holocaust Testimonies*, New Haven: Yale University Press.

Lees, S. (1993) *Sugar and Spice*, Harmondsworth: Penguin.

Linde, C. (1993) *Life Stories: The Creation of Coherence*, New York: Oxford University Press.

Lindesmith, A., Strauss, A. and Denzin, N. (1977) *Social Psychology*, Fifth Edition, New York: Holt, Rinehart and Winston.

MacIntyre A. (1981) *After Virtue*, London: Duckworth.

MacLachlan, G. and Reid, I. (1994) *Framing and Interpretation*, Melbourne: Melbourne University Press.

Maines, D. (1991) (ed.), *Social Organization and Social Process: Essays in Honor of Anselm Strauss*, New York: Aldine de Gruyter.

Markus, H. and Nurius, P. (1986) 'Possible Selves', *American Psychologist*, 41: 954-969.

Marsden, D. and Duff, E. (1975) *Workless*, Harmondsworth: Penguin.

Mattingly, C. (1994) 'The Concept of Therapeutic "Emplotment"', *Social Science and Medicine*, 38: 811-822.

McCall, G. and J. Simmons, (1966) *Identities and Interactions*, New York: The Free Press.

McDonald, K. (1994) 'On Work', *Arena Journal*, 2: 33-42.

McNamee, S. and Gergen, K. (1992) (eds) *Therapy as Social Construction*, London: Sage.

Mead, G. (1934) *Mind, Self and Society*, Chicago: University of Chicago Press.

Meaning of Work International Research Team, (1987) *The Meaning of Working*, London: Academic Press.

Merton, R. (1968) *Social Theory and Social Structure*, New York: Free Press.

Miles, M. and Huberman, A. (1994) *Qualitative Data Analysis*, Thousand Oaks: Sage.

Mills, C. (1970) *The Sociological Imagination*, Harmondsworth: Penguin.

Mishler, E. (1986) 'The Analysis of Interview Narratives', in T. Sarbin (ed.), *Narrative Psychology*, New York: Praeger.

Modell J. (1992) 'How do you introduce yourself as a childless mother?' in G. Rosenwald and R. Ochberg (eds), *Storied Lives*, New Haven: Yale University Press.

Nash, J. (1995) 'Post-Industrialism, Post-Fordism, and the Crisis in World Capitalism', in F. Gamst (ed.), *Meanings of Work*, New York: State University of New York Press.

Newton, T. (1996) 'Resocialising the subject? A re-reading of Grey's "Career as a project of the self ..."', *Sociology*, 30: 137-144.

O'Brien, G. (1985) 'Distortion in Unemployment Research: The Early Studies of Bakke and Their Implicatons for Current Research on Employment and Unemployment', *Human Relations*, 38: 877-894.

O'Brien, G. (1986) *Psychology of Work and Unemployment*, Chichester: John Wiley and Sons.

O'Brien, G. and Feather, N. (1990) The realtive effects of unemployment and quality of employment on the affect, work values and personal control of adolescents', *Journal of Occupational Psychology*, 63: 151-165.

Oatley, K and Bolton, W. (1985) 'A Socio-Cultural Theory of Depression in Reaction to Life Events', *Psychological Review*, 92: 372-388.

Ochberg, R. (1988) 'Life Stories and the Psychosocial Construction of Careers', *Journal of Personality*, 56: 175-204.

Offe, C. (1985) *Disorganised Capitalism*, Cambridge: Polity Press.

Pahl, R. (1984) *Divisons of Labour*, Oxford: Blackwell.

Pahl, R. (1995) *After Success: Fin-de-Siecle Anxiety and Identity*, Cambridge: Polity Press.

Parkes, C. (1985) 'Bereavement', *British Journal of Psychiatry*, 146: 11-17.

Parsons, T. (1951) *The Social System*, Glencoe, Ill.: Free Press.

Passerini, L. (1989) 'Women's Personal Narratives', in Personal Narratives Group (eds), *Interpreting Women's Lives*, Bloomington: Indiana University Press.

Payne, J. (1994) 'Book Review: Growing Up with Unemployment', *British Journal of Sociology*, 45: 712.

Pernice, R. (1996) 'Methodological issues in unemployment research', *Journal of Occupational and Organizational Psychology*, 69: 339-350.

Pixley, J. (1993) *Citizenship and Employment*, Melbourne: Cambridge University Press.

Polkinghorne, D. (1988) *Narrative Knowing and the Human Sciences*, New York: State University of New York Press.

Polkinghorne, D. (1991) 'Narrative and Self-Concept', *Journal of Narrative and Life History*, 1: 135-153.

Polonoff, D. (1987) 'Self-Deception', *Social Research*, 54: 45-53.

Potter, J. and Wetherell, M. (1987) *Discourse and Social Psychology*, London: Sage.

Pucci, E. (1992) 'Review of Paul Ricoeur's *Oneself as Another*', *Philosophy and Social Criticism*, 18: 185-209.

Rasmussen, D. (1995) 'Rethinking subjectivity: narrative identity and the self', *Philosophy and Social Criticism*, 21: 159-172.

Rice, P. and Ezzy, D. (1999) *Qualitative Research Methods: A Health Focus*, Melbourne: Oxford University Press.

Ricoeur, P. (1984) *Time and Narrative*, Volume 1, trans. K. McLaughlin & D. Pellauer, Chicago: University of Chicago Press.

Ricoeur, P. (1985) *Time and Narrative*, Volume 2, trans. K. McLaughlin & D. Pellauer, Chicago: University of Chicago Press.

Ricoeur, P. (1988) *Time and Narrative*, Volume 3, trans. K. Blamey & D. Pellauer, Chicago: University of Chicago Press.

Ricoeur, P. (1991a) 'Narrative Identity', trans. D. Wood in D. Wood (ed.), *On Paul Ricoeur*, London: Routledge.

Ricoeur, P. (1991b) 'Life in Quest of Narrative', trans. D. Wood in D. Wood (ed.), *On Paul Ricoeur*, London: Routledge.

Ricoeur, P. (1992) *Oneself as Another*, trans. K. Blamey, Chicago: University of Chicago Press.

Riemann, G. and F. Schutze (1991) '"Trajectory" as a basic theoretical concept for analyzing suffering and disorderly social process', in D. Maines (ed.), *Social*

Organization and Social Process: Essays in Honor of Anselm Strauss, New York: Aldine De Gruyter.

Riessman, C. (1993) *Narrative Analysis,* Newbury Park: Sage.

Riley, J. (1983) 'Dying and the Meanings of Death: Sociological Inquiries', *Annual Review of Sociology*, 9: 191-216.

Ritzer, G. (1981) 'The Failure to Integrate Theory and Practice: The Case of the Sociology of Work', *Journal of Applied Behavioural Science*, 17: 376-379.

Ritzer, G. (1995) *Expressing America*, Thousand Oaks: Pine Forge Press.

Robinson, J and Hawpe, L. (1986) 'Narrative Thinking as a Heuristic Process', in T. Sarbin (ed.), *Narrative Psychology*, New York: Praeger.

Rodriguez, Y. (1997) 'Learned helplessness or expectancy-value?' *Journal of Adolescence*, 20: 321-332.

Rose, N. (1989) *Governing the soul: The shaping of the private self*, London: Routledge.

Rosenberg, M. (1979) *Conceiving the Self*, New York: Basic Books.

Rosenwald, G. (1992) 'Conclusion: Reflection on Narrative Self-Understanding', in G. Rosenwald and R. Ochberg (eds), *Storied Lives*, New Haven: Yale University Press.

Rosenwald, G. and Ochberg, R. (1992) (eds), *Storied Lives: The Cultural Politics of Self-Understanding*, New Haven and London: Yale University Press.

Rowley, K. and Feather, N. (1987) 'The impact of unemployment in relation to age and length of unemployment', *Jornal of Occupational Psychology*, 60: 323-332.

Rundell, J. (1995) 'Gadamer and the Circles of Hermeneutics', in D. Roberts (ed.), *Reconstructing Theory*, Melbourne: Melbourne University Press.

Sarbin, T. and Kitsuse, J. (1994) (eds) *Constructing the Social*, London: Sage.

Scheff, T. (1991) *Microsociology*, Chicago: University of Chicago Press.

Scholes, R. and Kellogg, R. (1966) *The Nature of Narrative*, New York: Oxford University Press.

Seabrook, J. (1982) *Unemployment*, London: Quartet Books.

Simmel, G. (1990) *The Philsophy of Money*, trans. T. Bottomore and D. Frisby, London: Routledge.

Sinfield, A. (1981) *What Unemployment Means*, Oxford: Martin Robertson.

Smelt, S. (1980) 'Money's Place in Society', *British Journal of Sociology*, 31: 204-223.

Solt, A and S. Egan, (1988) *Imagine: John Lennon*, London: Bloomsbury.

Somers, M. (1994) 'The narrative constitution of identity', *Theory and Society*, 23: 605-649.

Somers, M. and Gibson, G. (1994) 'Reclaming the Epistemological "Other"', in C. Calhoun (ed.), *Social Theory and the Politics of Identity*, Oxford: Blackwell.

Spence, D. (1988) 'Tough and Tender-minded hermeneutics', in S. Messer, L. Saas, R. Woolfolk (eds), *Hermeneutics and Psychological Theory*, New Brunswick and London: Rutgers University Press.

Stokes, G and Cochrane, R. (1984) 'A study of the psychological effects of redundance and unemployment', *Journal of Occupational Psychology*, 57: 309-322.

Strauss, A. (1969) *Mirrors and Masks*, London: Martin Robertson.

Strauss, A. (1970) 'Discovering New Theory from Previous Theory', in T. Shibutani (ed.), *Human Nature and Collective Behavior*, New Jersey: Prentice Hall.

Strauss, A and Corbin, J. (1990) *Basics of Qualitative Research*, London: Sage.

Sykes, G. and Matza, D. (1957) 'On Neutralizing Delinquent Self-images', *American Sociological Review*, 22: 667-670.

Taylor, C. (1989) *Sources of the Self*, Cambridge: Cambridge University Press.

Taylor, F. (1913) *The Principles of Scientific Management*, New York: Harper.

Thoits, P. (1985) 'Self-labeling Process in Mental Illness: the Role of Emotional Deviance', *American Journal of Sociology*, 91: 221-244.

Thomas, W. (1928) *The Child In America*, New York: Knopf.

Tiffany, D., Cowan, J. and Tiffany, P. (1970) *The Unemployed: A Social Psychological Portrait*, New Jersey: Prentice Hall.

Turner, J. (1987) 'Toward a Sociological Theory of Motivation', *American Sociology Review*, 52: 15-27.

Turner, M. (1983) *Stuck! Unemployed people talk to Michele Turner*, Melbourne: Penguin.

Turner, R. (1972) 'The Role and the Person', *American Journal of Sociology*, 84: 1-23.

Turner, R. (1976) 'The Real Self: From Institution to Impulse', *American Journal of Sociology*, 81: 989-1016.

Turner, R., Bostyn, A., Wight, D. (1984) 'The work ethic in a Scottish town with declining employment', in B. Roberts, R. Finnegan and D. Gallie (eds), *New Approaches to Economic Life*, Manchester: Manchester University Press.

Turner, R. and Schutte, J. (1981) 'The True Self Method for Studying the Self-Conception', *Symbolic Interaction*, 4: 1-20.

Turner, V. (1969) *The Ritual Process*, New York: Cornell University Press.

Van Gennep, A. (1977), *The Rites of Passage*, trans. M. Vizedom and G. Caffee, London and Henley: Routledge and Kegan Paul.

Van Manen, M. (1990) *Researching Lived Experience*, New York: State University of New York Press.

Walker, A., Noble, I. and Westergaard, J. (1984) 'From secure employment to labour market insecurity: the impact of redundancy on older workers in the steel industry', in B. Roberts, R. Finnegan and D. Gallie (eds), *New Approaches to Economic Life*, Manchester: Manchester University Press.

Warr, P. (1984) 'Twelve questions about unemployment and health', in B. Roberts, R. Finnegan and D. Gallie (eds), *New Approaches to Economic Life*, Manchester: Manchester University Press.

Warr, P. (1987) *Work, Unemployment and Mental Health*, Oxford: Clarendon Press.

Warr, P and Jackson, P. (1983). 'Self-esteem and unemployment among young workers', *Le Travail Humain*, 46: 335-366.

Warr, P. and Jackson, P. (1984) 'Men without jobs: Some correlates of age and length of unemployment', *Journal of Occupational Psychology*, 57: 77-85.

White, H. (1973) *Metahistory*, Baltimore: The Johns Hopkins University Press.

White, M. (1992) 'Deconstruction and Therapy', in Epston, D. and White, M. (1992) *Experience, Contradiction, Narrative and Imagination*, South Australia: Dulwich Centre Publications.

Whyte W. (1956) *The Organization Man*, New York: Simon and Schuster.

Wiersma, J. (1992) 'Karen: The Transforming Story', in G. Rosenwald and R. Ochberg (eds), *Storied Lives*, New Haven: Yale University Press.

Williams, C. (1992) *Beyond Industrial Sociology*, Sydney: Allen and Unwin.

Willmott, H. (1990) 'Subjectivity and the Dialectics of Praxis', in D. Knights and H. Willmott (eds), *Labour Process Theory*, London: Macmillan.

Wilson, B. and Wyn, J. (1987) *Shaping Futures,* Sydney: Allen and Unwin.

Winefield, A. (1995) 'Unemployment: Its Psychological Costs', *International Review of Industrial and Organizational Psychology*, vol. 10: 169-212.

Winefield, A., Tiggemann, M. and Winefield, H. (1990) 'Factors moderating the psychological impact of unemployment at different ages', *Personality and Individual Differences*, 11: 45-52.

Winefield, A., Tiggeman, M., Winefield, H. and Goldney, R. (1993) *Growing Up with Unemployment*, London: Routledge.

Zelizer, V. (1994) *The Social Meaning of Money,* New York: Basic Books.

Index